Sidewalking

The publisher gratefully acknowledges the generous support of the Lisa See Endowment Fund in Southern California History and Culture of the University of California Press Foundation.

Sidewalking

Coming to Terms with Los Angeles

David L. Ulin

UNIVERSITY OF CALIFORNIA PRESS

University of California Press, one of the most distinguished university presses in the United States, enriches lives around the world by advancing scholarship in the humanities, social sciences, and natural sciences. Its activities are supported by the UC Press Foundation and by philanthropic contributions from individuals and institutions. For more information, visit www.ucpress.edu.

University of California Press
Oakland, California

Library of Congress Cataloging-in-Publication Data

Ulin, David L., author.
    Sidewalking : coming to terms with Los Angeles / David L. Ulin.
        p.   cm.
    ISBN 978-0-520-27372-6 (cloth : alk. paper)
    ISBN 978-0-520-96309-2 (ebook)
        1. Streets—California—Los Angeles.   2. Walking—California—Los Angeles.
3. Los Angeles (Calif.)—Description and travel.   I. Title.
    F869.L875A27   2015
    917.94′94—dc23   2015010041

Manufactured in the United States of America

24 23 22 21 20 19 18 17 16 15
10 9 8 7 6 5 4 3 2 1

The paper used in this publication meets the minimum requirements of ANSI/NISO Z39.48–1992 (R 2002) (*Permanence of Paper*).

For Noah, fellow traveler . . .

There it is. Take it.

William Mulholland

CONTENTS

ACKNOWLEDGMENTS

I began to write about Los Angeles in the 1980s, when I still lived in New York. Back then, I thought it would be easy to understand. Naïveté, yes, but also my first experience of L.A.'s elusiveness, the illusion of its glittering surfaces, which distract us from its elemental realities. I have lived here since 1991 and have spent much of that time trying to make sense of the city—or to make sense of it for *me*.

Sidewalking is a record of those attempts at sense-making, although it is more a set of impressions than a narrative. Los Angeles, after all, resists narrative, or at least master narrative; we are always making it up as we go along. Think of this book, then, as one individual's sequence of associations, defined as much by who I am, by what I want, as by the ways in which the city asserts itself.

That being said, there are many people to thank, beginning with the writers who helped unlock the city and its identity for me. Louis Adamic, Carey McWilliams, Joan Didion, Mike

Davis, Norman M. Klein—that great contrarian strain of Southern California commentators: my heroes, my heritage. Reading their work, I came to understand the complexities of this landscape, its peculiar fingerprints of place. So, too, Reyner Banham, whose *Los Angeles: The Architecture of Four Ecologies* remains a touchstone text, the reflections of another transplant who (as they say) went native, like the palm trees and, in a certain sense, myself. And, of course, all those who opened themselves up to my questions and investigations: Eric Brightwell, Diego Cardoso, Rick Caruso, Robbert Flick, Michael Govan, Greg Hise, and Rebecca Solnit.

I especially want to thank Alice Kimm and the students of our Spring 2014 "Literature and the Urban Experience" course at the University of Southern California's School of Architecture. Our in-class conversation functioned as a kind of incubator for many of the ideas discussed in the book. I'd also like to thank the Henry E. Huntington Library, in San Marino, California, for a 2009 John Randolph Haynes and Dora Haynes Foundation Fellowship, which provided early research funding and support. And I owe a particular debt to Leah and Ra'anan Boustan for their generosity and hospitality in sharing Eric Brightwell's map of Miracle Mile.

In addition, I would like to thank Jon Christensen, Bill Deverell, Lynell George, Christopher Hawthorne, Carolyn Kellogg, Terry Morello, Miriam Pawel, Richard Rayner, Carolyn See, and Mark Haskell Smith—for friendship, conversation, and invaluable assistance in clarifying my thinking, or my confusions, about L.A. My thanks also to Kim Robinson, friend and editor at the University of California Press, and my agent, Bonnie Nadell, for their intelligence and support.

Most of all, there's my wife, Rae Dubow, who has been the catalyst for so much, including our move to Southern California, and our children, Noah and Sophie—my two Angelenos, I once referred to them. You are my heart, my life, the measure of my breathing. My gratitude for your fierce and tender love.

Street, Haunting

The eye is not a miner, not a diver, not a seeker after buried treasure. It floats us smoothly down a stream.

Virginia Woolf

There is a church I like on Cochran Avenue. Little street-corner church, adobe-style, like a mission in some minor key. I discovered it during a walk in the neighborhood, one of the interminable loops by which I mark my place in this city, east on Packard out to Cochran, south toward Pico and back around, the whole thing one vast circle, a walkabout, a songline, a way to meander my universe into being. Then one afternoon, I broke the pattern and rather than heading south, I went north, where I found the church. "This morning, going against all convention, I turned right instead of left," Sven Birkerts writes in *The Other Walk*, describing his own inadvertent rewiring of a common saunter. "Going against the grain of my usual track, seeing every single thing from the other side, was suddenly welcome." Suddenly welcome, yes, but also—for me, at least—a means of turning the walk into a journey of discovery again. We walk, or *I* do, to pay attention, to see the streets, the buildings that surround us, to immerse ourselves in a world that might otherwise slip by. And yet, the paradox is that the more we walk, the less we notice, the more the passing landscape blurs to indistinction, like the backdrop in a *Road Runner* cartoon. That's especially true of Los Angeles, this thirty-five-mile-per-hour city, where the very notion of the street as public space remains alien somehow. I think of Joan Didion: "A good part of any day in Los Angeles is spent driving, alone, through streets devoid of meaning to the driver, which is one reason the place exhilarates some people, and floods others with an amorphous unease." She's right, of course, although what she neglects to say is just how institutionalized this process is, in a city where we can leave our homes and drive to work, to dinner, to the movies without ever stepping outside.

Anyway, the church. I fell for it from the moment I saw it, on the corner of Cochran and Packard, built into the slow slope of a hill. There was the dome of the bell tower, faded gilt, stained glass windows brown as mica, the building stretching back half a block or so, deceptive in its depth. Even more, there was the way it fit into the neighborhood—or not the neighborhood, exactly, but the block. East of the church on Cochran was what looked like a low-slung rectory, and just beyond that, a two-story apartment house, eight units maybe, pallid stucco, flat and hulking, with a red tile roof. All three buildings looked as though they'd been put up in the 1930s, that golden age of California urban architecture, utilitarian and beautiful at once. This is the California of my first infatuation, imprinted when I was eighteen and living in San Francisco, a city I once wandered like a mendicant, memorizing its sidewalks through the soles of my feet. I remember coming across block after block much like this one: apartments next to street-corner churches. In San Francisco, the buildings were bigger, four or five stories, and cleaner, framing the Marina or Pacific Heights in blinding white. Still, there was something about *this* streetscape, its whisper of density, which brought me back to all those peregrinations through that other city, the randomness, the serendipity of urban space. Above the buildings, the sky was hooded, overcast, San Francisco weather, as if a fog were moving in. If I squinted, I could almost see it, one city bleeding through another, an imago, an unexpected trace.

This is what I love about cities, the way that even the most distinct of them resemble one another when you least expect it, the way the lines between memory and imagination blur. When I was a kid listening to my grandfather reminisce about the glory days of Flatbush, I used to regret, with a child's peculiar secondhand nostalgia, everything I thought I'd missed. Then I moved, in 1991, to Los Angeles, the Fairfax district, where, the first time she came to visit, my mother declared with a mix of dismay and disbelief: "You've moved to Brooklyn in the 1940s." She was referring to the shabby duplexes, the delis and the kosher bakeries, all the black hats on Fairfax and the side streets, with their *tefillin* and their prayers. For me, however, it was a different kind of lens through which to reckon with the past. L.A. even had the Dodgers, a defining aspect of my grandfather's Brooklyn, and if there was little happening at Dodger Stadium that recalled the teams that had played at Ebbets Field, there it was in any case: another echo, another rhyme. "When I go down Figueroa," Norman Klein once told me, as we ate at a taqueria in his neighborhood of Highland Park, "I literally flash back to my teenage years on Avenue U in South Brooklyn.... Even though the people here are Salvadoran, I can almost see them as Jewish. I find this a lot." What he meant was that, in his eyes, Los Angeles was less a unified city than "a collection of microclimates, of ethnicity and layers of urban traces, one upon the other"—which, whatever else it signifies, renders the place a template for our fantasies. In *The History of Forgetting*, Klein makes the point explicit, citing the city's history of serving as informal film set, often dressed up to resemble *somewhere else*. "I am not implying," he writes, "that L.A.'s neighborhoods have no public record at all; quite the contrary. The photo archives of vernacular Los Angeles are indeed gigantic, running into millions of images.... However, these cannot compete with hundreds of movie melodramas where downtown is a backdrop.... Some locations are simply easier to transfigure than others, for heavy equipment to be positioned, or cheaper to rent; and they therefore figure more powerfully in the public record, while others never appear. Indeed, Los Angeles remains the most photographed and least remembered city in the world."

Most photographed, least remembered. The difference is between a public and a private record, between a city's outer and its inner life. This is why I walk, to root myself, to create a space, a history, a language. I walk to remember, in other words, not to forget. Yet Klein's "vernacular Los Angeles" suggests a subtext in which the city may emerge as a set of snapshots, a survey of small moments, L.A. as *environment* rather than as sprawl or backdrop, reconnoitered at the level of its streets. As soon as I saw the church, I pulled out my cell phone and started shooting, first the building, then a series of long, angled takes down the sidewalk, an attempt to capture the length of the block. There was something here I didn't want to let slip, some juxtaposition of angles, a way their composition seemed to bring me closer to myself. I couldn't explain it then, and I can't explain it now, couldn't explain it moments later when the pastor came outside to see what I was doing, a tall black man in a white shirt, who introduced himself and tried to draw me into conversation, telling me about the church school and its calling *("where the mission of Christ is meeting the needs of the people")*, theology as social justice, theology as community. I stood there on the sidewalk and listened, by turns sympathetic and unsympathetic, a believer in social justice, in community, if not quite so much in theology. I nodded politely when he invited me to come back for a service, murmured something vague and indistinct. How could I tell him that what had drawn me was not the message—not the *overt* message, anyway—but a sensation more elusive, the idea of these buildings as a kind of hieroglyphic spelled out against the ledger of the street? How could I tell him that I'd stopped because his church was both familiar and utterly unfamiliar, that, in some odd way, I felt I knew it, even though I'd never seen it before? Echoes again, imagoes, resonances ... all of it, yes, a reflection of the serendipity of the streets.

Were all this taking place in another city, it would hardly seem remarkable, all these whispers, all these ghosts. A few months later, I was wandering the Upper West Side of Manhattan when it hit me: the city as if not necropolis then imaginatorium, where the surface, *the public record*, is constantly collapsing into the interior landscape, the streets as markers, territorial or otherwise, the building blocks, the triggers, of identity. This is why Aboriginals go on walkabout; this is the essence of their Dreaming tracks. And in Manhattan, where I was raised, and where I lived—with the exception of my time in San Francisco, as well as several loose years in and around Philadelphia and Boston—until I was nearly thirty, those tracks for me are deep, trenches really, with the present always, *always*, burrowed by the past. When I walk New York, I walk my way back into my childhood, into my adolescence, into the early days of my adulthood: I see my life pass through those streets. Or *pieces* of my life, depending on the neighborhood, and nowhere more than on the Upper West Side. This is important, the New York version of Birkerts's turning right instead of left, for there is little recent history in that corner of the borough to overlay my early tracks. The Upper East Side, Midtown, Lower Manhattan: that's where I visit when I'm in New York, where I lived and worked and where I continue to have an ongoing engagement, a relationship with the city, if such a thing is even possible in a city where one no longer lives. The Upper West Side, however, stands apart. Although I was born there, and spent time there again in my early twenties, after my future wife, Rae, moved into a studio on West Seventieth Street, I'm never on those sidewalks now. When Rae lived in the neighborhood, working at an Irish pub on Columbus Avenue, my grandparents were around the corner, exiled from Brooklyn to West End Avenue, in a massive apartment block at right angles to the Hudson, as blank as a tombstone scoured clean by wind. Until 1998, the year my grandmother died in that building, I dutifully went back every six or nine or twelve months to pay my dues, pay my respects, pay it forward, pay it out. And then she was gone, and for me, it was as if the neighborhood had ceased existing, as if it were not part of Manhattan anymore.

Because of this, perhaps, when I found myself on the Upper West Side, killing time in the early evening before going to a party, it felt different in some quantifiable way from the walks I usually take when I'm in New York. This was history, pure and simple, a trench with nothing else outside it, as recognizable and unrecognizable as that adobe-style street-corner church. And yet, unlike on Cochran Avenue, the echoes here were not of another city but of these very sidewalks, of experiences long since left behind. On Columbus Avenue, I stopped briefly outside the pub where Rae had waited tables, took a photo with my cell phone, peeked through the front window at the bar. For a moment, I considered stopping in, but something held me back, a sense not of connection but of detachment, of time less in suspension than in relentless movement, the understanding that, beneath its superficial familiarity, the place had irrevocably changed. This is the most obvious idea in the world, that time takes everything from us, that the streets feel possessed by ghosts because they *are* possessed by ghosts, the ghosts of all the people who have ever traversed them, who have ever occupied those cubic feet of space. But it is more than that also, more personal, more … evocative is one way of putting it but not the right one, suggesting as it does a consolation I don't really feel. No, more accurate to think in terms of lostness, melancholy, a fluid (dis)association, a way the streets remind us of how impossibly distant even the most immediate memories are. "The past is never dead," William Faulkner wrote in *Requiem for a Nun*. "It's not even past." He's right, of course, in the sense that we never escape our history, although it's equally the case that the past can't be reclaimed. This is the appeal of photographs, that vernacular public record: they operate as windows, allowing us to see, almost to enter, what would otherwise be lost. And yet, the key word there is *almost*, since no matter how a photo moves us, it also leaves us feeling disconnected, as I was left by the front window at that Irish bar. I could look, but there was something in the place that prevented me from touching, that prevented me from stepping inside the frame.

This push and pull, this *(yes)* amorphous unease, deepened as I left the bar, turning from Columbus onto West Seventieth Street, sliding past Rae's old building, across Broadway and down the long sloping block towards West End. To my left, a

schoolyard, empty in the darkness; up ahead, the building where
my grandparents once lived. In the density of evening, it looked
conditional, poorly constructed, a series of concrete slabs inter-
posed with light. I could almost smell the stale air of the long
corridors, bound on all sides by apartment doors, feel the rattle
of the elevator twenty-nine floors up, the metallic click as we
passed each landing, the whine of the engine as we rose. In front
of the entrance, a family walked in the direction of the river—or
not the river, not any longer, but a street that had not been here
fifteen years ago. *Freedom Place*, the sign read, and then a clutch
of buildings, towering over the West Side Highway, a former
industrial block gone residential, all part of the process by which
the city reinvents itself. I looked at the building, tried to imagine
the old apartment, who lived there, what they knew. I wondered
what would happen if I went inside and asked to see it, yet I
knew I never would. There were ghosts here, but only in the
merest sense; I might walk half a block, to Freedom Place, and
be in a New York I had never seen. I stood for a moment, more
adrift than actually remembering, then turned right instead of
left and sidled up to West Seventy-first Street, where I turned
right again and reentered Manhattan as I know it: hundred-
year-old apartment buildings, five and six stories, brick and
scrollwork, garbage cans clustered at the stoops. Ahead of me, a
woman spoke Spanish into a cell phone; otherwise, the sidewalk
was deserted, dark. It could have been any moment in my life or
any other—a generic streetscape rendered specific by the sheer
fact of my presence, the associations this stirred. I thought of
movies I'd seen, movies shot when I was growing up in the city,
the crumbling rape light clarity of 1970s New York. *Serpico, Dog
Day Afternoon, Death Wish* ... didn't Charles Bronson's vigilante
architect Paul Kersey take his vengeance around here? Or no,

I thought, as suddenly I saw it, Martin Scorsese in the back of Travis Bickle's taxi, pointing at a lit window on the second floor. "*You see the light up there, the window?*" he asks, voice a cascade of falling marbles, and then, "*That's my wife. But it's not my apartment.*" Not my apartment. No, nor my apartment either. Not in this neighborhood, not in this city, not anymore.

It's ironic, I suppose, that I should frame New York through the lens of movies, since I almost never think of Los Angeles that way. Nor, for that matter, do I think of it in terms of loss—at least, not of the generational kind. In Los Angeles, I don't have the history, the accumulation of collective memory: I've only lived here for twenty-one years. That's the age of majority, as I joked to someone recently, but I remember how young I was at twenty-one, how inexperienced, which makes that span of time a metaphor also, both for the city, which is still in its own slow process of becoming, and for my elliptical relationship to it, my attempt to find among its streets and sidewalks a place I might recognize as home. This, in turn, brings me back to why I walk here, as an act of creation, of *mutual* creation, in which I remake L.A. in my image (or the image of every other city I've ever inhabited, those ghosts, those echoes) even as it remakes me. I live in Los Angeles not as an Angeleno—that is, a native—but as a lifer, an exile, no matter how familiar my exile becomes. "It occurs to her," Kate Braverman writes in *Palm Latitudes*, a novel published at the very moment I was first seriously considering a move to Southern California, "that what she most appreciates about this City of Angels is that which is missing, the voids, the unstitched borders, the empty corridors, the not yet deciphered. She is grateful for the absence of history." Yes, yes, although in the absence of history, we have no choice but to interpose our own. I walk here because I have always walked in cities. I walk to bring my history to life. And when, on one occasion or another, I turn right instead of left and stumble upon a church I've never seen before, I walk a line between this city as it is and *as it is to me*, haunted, haunting, fraught with association, between what I know and what I might have otherwise passed by.

Los Angeles Plays Itself

I want to live in Los Angeles, but not the one in Los
Angeles.

Frank Black

One night not so very long ago, I went to visit a friend who lives
in West Hollywood. This used to be an easy drive: a geometry
of short, straight lines from my home in the Mid-Wilshire
flats—west on Olympic to Crescent Heights, north past Santa
Monica Boulevard. Yet like everywhere these days, it seems,
Los Angeles is no longer the place it used to be. Over the past
decade and a half, the city has densified: building up and not
out, erecting more malls, more apartment buildings, more high-
rises. At the same time, gridlock has grown increasingly terminal, and so, even well after rush hour on a weekday evening, I
found myself boxed in and looking for a shortcut, which, in an
automotive culture such as this one, means a whole new way of
conceptualizing urban space.

There are those (myself among them) who would argue that
the very act of living in L.A. requires an ongoing process of
reconceptualization, of rethinking not just the place but also our
relationship to it, our sense of what it means. As much as any

city, Los Angeles is a work-in-progress, a landscape of fragments where the boundaries we take for granted in other environments are not always clear. You can see this in the most unexpected locations, from Rick Caruso's Grove to the Los Angeles County Museum of Art, where Chris Burden's sculpture *Urban Light*—a cluster of 202 working vintage lampposts—fundamentally changed the nature of Wilshire Boulevard when it was installed in 2008. Until then, the museum (like so much of L.A.) had resisted the street, the pedestrian, in the most literal way imaginable, presenting a series of walls to the sidewalk, its cavernous entry recessed into the middle of a long, imposing block. Burden intended to create a catalyst, a provocation. "I've been driving by these buildings for forty years, and it's always bugged me how this institution turned its back on the city," he told the *Los Angeles Times* one week before his project was lit. When I first came to Los Angeles a quarter of a century ago, the area around the County Museum was seedy; it's no coincidence that in the film *Grand Canyon*, Mary Louise Parker gets held up at gunpoint just a few short streets away. Take a walk down Wilshire now, however, and you'll find different sorts of interactions: food trucks, pedestrians, tourists, people from the neighborhood.

Perhaps only in Los Angeles would this feel like a revolution: a street with a culture unto itself. But then, L.A. may be unique among American cities for having lost sight of its boulevards as public space. Its self-image has long been one of cool containment, the autopia of Reyner Banham and Cees Nooteboom. This is a city where the most basic cornerstones are understood to be private—private life, private architecture—a city Louis Adamic once described as "the enormous village," where the single-family house is the essential heart. And yet, in contemporary Los Angeles that is changing, as population growth forces our hand. What is the great civic projects of the twenty-first century? Light rail, subways, bike lanes, a transportation network in which the one-car-one-commuter ethos is replaced by something more inclusive, an infrastructure that reflects less how the city may once have seen itself than what it has become.

The irony, of course, is that such a perspective is (has always been) encoded into L.A.'s history, which means that we look forward by looking back. A hundred years ago, the Pacific Electric Railroad, better known as the Red Car, offered Angelenos the world's largest interurban public transit system, with more than two thousand trains and a thousand miles of track stretching as far as San Bernardino and Redlands. It's been half a century since those trains ran anywhere other than a mile-and-a-half tourist loop at the San Pedro waterfront—I rode them there once, with my children—although there has been noise for almost a generation about bringing some version of them back to downtown. As recently as 2006, the now-defunct Community Redevelopment Agency was doing feasibility studies about running vintage streetcars "to create a tourist attraction of historical significance which would also provide an additional means of transportation much like the cable cars and the Market Street Railway in San Francisco," which averages twenty-thousand riders daily, many of them visitors traveling between Fisherman's Wharf and the Castro on a fleet of throwback trains. Some of those San Francisco trolleys, PCC-brand streetcars from the 1930s, 1940s, and 1950s, are painted to look like L.A. Red Cars: another irony, since the downtown trolley, if it ever gets completed, will no longer be a vintage line. Go to the project's website, and you'll find a computer-generated image of a hypermodern car, green and blue, streamlined as a bullet, with the tower of the Marriott in the background, and a cyclist, wearing helmet and backpack, passing alongside.

Here we have a vision of the new Los Angeles, eco-friendly and sustainable, in which downtown is transformed into an emblem of the future and not of the past. Is it cynical of me to say that this is as it should be, yet another example of the city's faith in reinvention, the idea that the past is a blank slate and the future its own kind of fantasy? "Nothing dies in California," the poet William Everson once observed; "it is the land of non-death.... There is no intrinsic knowledge in the sense of locality—our graveyards have been built within living memory." Our graveyards, and our cities too. The current downtown revival is at least the third since I first started coming to L.A. in the 1980s, and if it looks like it is taking hold this time, it is not without its stumbles, its false steps. The downtown trolley may end up as one of them: underfunded, behind schedule, it remains more conditional than it should be, a desire if not quite a plan. Click through the website and the only links are to Facebook and Twitter, neither of which have been updated in any serious way for months.

But don't get me wrong. This tension between past and future is precisely what draws me to downtown, where the old and new cities circle back on one another like an ouroboros. I am pulled, in other words, by the way history in these blocks exists just below the surface, a hidden language we must teach ourselves to read. For a long time, downtown was an enigma to me, an emblem of the dreamlike, floating quality of Los Angeles. On one of my early visits, five years before I moved to California, I spent a week with a friend and, every day, was driven somewhere in his convertible—to a restaurant, to a bookstore, to the movies, to the beach. That passive framing is essential, since I had no agency. I would sit in the passenger seat, staring at the soft parade of streets and structures, the bungalows and palm trees, postage stamp lawns and stucco storefronts, all of it as indistinct as a film set, as if joined to no underlying narrative. I remember that I kept asking where downtown was, as if this might somehow root me; little did I realize that for many Angelenos) downtown (then and even now) glittered in the distance like the Emerald City, center as illusion, as the place we never reach. Half a decade later, on my first foray as a resident, I set out to cross, against the lights, an empty boulevard (Grand Avenue? Olive Street? I have a vague memory of passing in front of the Biltmore, by the big front doors where the Black Dahlia was seen alive for the last time) only to be berated by another pedestrian. "Oh, I see," she called scornfully, "we're playing by New York rules today." If I am to be honest, it was the New Yorkiness of these streets, with their turn-of-the-last-century architecture, ten- and twelve-story buildings of brick and cornices, that was part of the attraction, a cityscape that was (at least) visually recognizable, even if the sidewalks remained as empty as the aftermath of a neutron bomb. Or no, not only that, this wishful familiarity, but also the exoticism of a city that didn't fit my preconceptions, that played by a different set of imperatives. In the film *Wolf,* we watch as Jack Nicholson wanders down lower Broadway in Manhattan, only to find ourselves, once he steps inside his company's headquarters, on an altogether different Broadway, in the lobby of the Bradbury building in downtown L.A. It is, to be sure, a clumsy bit of movie magic, especially for anyone familiar with both locations, but at the same time, perhaps it suggests a way of reflecting on place and how we interact with it, a lens on what it does and does not mean.

The Bradbury, after all, is one of Los Angeles's finest landmarks, a five-story gem of a building erected at the corner of Third and Broadway in 1893, when the city's population was in the range of sixty thousand, although downtown was already (relatively) urbanized. In an 1889 photo, taken to mark the opening of the Downey Avenue Cable Railroad, we see Broadway four years earlier: a wide street, somewhat sleepy, pocked with trolleys and horse-drawn carriages, horizon tapering off to flatness as the edges of the city assert themselves. Little more than a decade later, a 1902 shot of Spring Street looking south from First (the current location of the *Los Angeles Times* building) reveals a cityscape transformed. In the foreground, the Hotel Nadeau sits across from Western Union, and the pavement is cluttered with electric streetcars, at least seven I can count. There are, as before, horse-drawn surreys and hansom cabs, but now we see the first intrusion of the automobile. Buildings of five and six stories are not uncommon, and the sidewalks are dense with people walking, people standing, people talking, loitering, mostly men but a few women here and there. By 1909, a panoramic map reveals the configurations of the modern city: blocks of taller buildings (ten, twelve, fourteen floors) framing the urban core, factories and rail yards stretching along the river; by then, more than three hundred thousand people lived in L.A. The original name of Broadway, when it was still a dirt road in the years before Los Angeles began to play itself, was Eternity Street; it led, fittingly, to a cemetery. Such a resonance suggests an almost perfect symbol for the city and all its layered meanings, the way past and present intertwine at the level of forgetting, like a nineteenth-century graveyard in which the few remaining monuments insist that we remember we are part of something bigger than ourselves.

Such an interplay of present tense and history occurs, of course, in any downtown. One of the ideas I want to argue against is a sense of Los Angeles' exceptionalism, that this city is fundamentally different from any other, although in many ways it is. If that sounds like a contradiction, that is also part of the point. Los Angeles continually evades us (or evades me), forcing us to rethink what we take for granted about how it, how any city, works. This is why I both love and hate the place, source of my fascination and my resistance, my efforts to remake the city, or my experience of it, in a way I can recognize. Downtown is a perfect case in point. Once or twice a year, I lead a group of students on a walking tour intended to get at these very oppositions: not negations, exactly, but complications, struggles, inconsistencies. Like everything else in Los Angeles, pedestrianism comes with its own context, its own set of crisis points. Walking is a joke, a punch line, the lyric to a bad pop anthem: "Nobody walks in L.A.," sang Missing Persons' Dale Bozzio in 1982. Walking is a conundrum, a question mark. When I first began to think about walking in Los Angeles, a friend asked, "You're not going to make the case for L.A. as a walking city, are you?" It's an excellent question, one that (again) highlights the complexities, the ongoing tension between hype and what, for want of a better word, let's call reality.

According to a 2014 report by SmartGrowth America and George Washington University, Los Angeles is becoming more pedestrian; although it tied for sixteenth (with Kansas City and Columbus, Ohio) among thirty metropolitan areas in regard to walkability, "the future—of a walkable, transit-friendly Los Angeles—is being built right now." The future, yes, and also the past. To live here is to play an elaborate Situationist game of psychogeography, in which we displace ourselves by interposing the psychic map of one city over another city's terrain. Sometimes, this is the city in which we were raised, the city that imprinted us, which is why I have created in Los Angeles a lifestyle more suited to New York or San Francisco, walking to the bank, to the dry cleaner, to the grocery store, to a restaurant or coffee shop, to the La Brea Tar Pits and the County Museum. Sometimes, it is the city Los Angeles used to be. Here we see the appeal of downtown, which because of neglect, perhaps, and now also changing attitudes, holds the DNA of L.A., our collective heritage, at street level, if we know how to look. No, Los Angeles is not a walking city, to answer my friend's question, and despite the promise of the SmartGrowth America report. Any city where you have to drive to a pedestrian district cannot be called a walking city, no matter how much we might want it to be one. At the same time, we create, or recreate, public space to suit ourselves, to mirror our interior, our private lives. If we do it right, this allows us to discover something not only about who we are but also about where we live—how it is and how it once was, and how, we hope or wonder, it may one day become.

So I walk. I start at the top of Bunker Hill, cleared and flattened in the early 1960s, when derelict boarding houses and SROs made way for office towers, museums, and concert halls. I start at California Plaza, with its terraces and dancing waters, workers eating in the shadow of the former Deloitte and Touche building, the Angels Flight gateway just a short curve of steps away on the eastern summit of the slope. If I have students with me, we talk about the history of this hillside, first developed in the late 1860s as the residential heart of Los Angeles, where the Victorian homes of doctors, lawyers, business leaders and their families sat clustered—the Beverly Hills of the nineteenth century. By the 1890s, apartment buildings had begun to rise among the mansions; you can see them in an 1895 photo taken from the tower of the old city hall. Half a decade later, the city dug the Third Street Tunnel (which, more than a century later, still looks as it did then), and a year after that, Angels Flight opened, running uphill at a thirty-three degree grade for two blocks alongside the tunnel at the intersection of Third and Hill Streets, where it remained in continuous operation for sixty-eight years. It has been called "The World's Shortest Railway," although it's more potent as a symbol of how Los Angeles doubles back on itself. Originally built to allow Bunker Hill's professional class to travel more easily between home and work, Angels Flight was closed in 1969 and became a different sort of attraction when it reopened in 1996, after twenty-seven years in storage, half a block south of its original location … a model, perhaps, for the unbuilt downtown trolley, by turns throwback and curiosity, a mechanism for tracing a through line between present and past. Or maybe not: in 2001, the funicular closed for nine years after a fatal accident, then closed again in 2013, because of safety violations. It has not returned to service since.

The same might be said of Bunker Hill. "No more perfect petrification of the '90s and early 1900s could be found in any western American city, not even in San Francisco, where they cherish, even reverence, mustiness. In Los Angeles, the spanking new is reverenced, and Bunker Hill was only tolerated, for the most part ignored," Timothy G. Turner observed in *Turn Off the Sunshine: Tales of Los Angeles on the Wrong Side of the Tracks*, published in 1942. The assessment brings to mind John Fante, whose 1939 novel *Ask the Dust* remains as unrelenting a portrait of desire and desperation as exists in L.A.'s literature. "Dust and old buildings and old people sitting at windows," Fante writes, describing the desolation of Bunker Hill, "old people tottering out of doors, old people moving painfully along the dark street. The old folk from Indiana and Iowa and Illinois, from Boston and Kansas City and Des Moines, they sold their homes and their stores, and they came here by train and by automobile to the land of sunshine, to die in the sun, with just enough money to live until the sun killed them, tore themselves out by the roots in their last days, deserted the smug prosperity of Kansas City and Chicago and Peoria to find a place in the sun." Early in *Ask the Dust*, Fante's protagonist, a young writer named Arturo Bandini, describes seeing his first palm tree, that powerful, if false, emblem of Southern California's exotic promise. (Only the California fan palm is indigenous to the state; every other palm species came here from somewhere else.) "Sure enough," Bandini tells us, "I thought of Palm Sunday and Egypt and Cleopatra, but the palm was blackish at its branches, stained by carbon monoxide coming out of the Third Street Tunnel, its crusted trunk choked with dust and sand that blew in from the Mojave and Santa Ana deserts." A generation later, we find a similar sensibility in Kent Mackenzie's 1961 film *The Exiles*, which evokes the last days of the old Bunker Hill, before the razing and the flattening and the renewal, before the reimagining of history as expression of corporate space. The movie is a hybrid of documentary and drama, a night-in-the-life story of young Native Americans living in the neighborhood, and it offers, as Thom Andersen points out in his own film *Los Angeles Plays Itself*, "a remarkable record of a city that has vanished."

Is it a stretch to look for all this underneath the glittery surfaces of California Plaza's pools and fountains? The answer is yes and no. Yes, because how much does the past, really, infuse our experience of the present? No, because it is perhaps the only way meaning accrues. What does it mean that Los Angeles has a history we can walk through, albeit a history that few seem willing, or able, to recognize? On the most essential terms, it restates the tension between L.A. as concrete and as elusive, between the city as a real place and as a kind of fever dream.

I confront the residue of this conflict everywhere; I don't even have to look that hard. This is the story of Angels Flight, which was shuttered, moved, and resurrected—with no sense of dislocation or even irony. It is the story of Chinatown, razed to make room for Union Station and then established in its current location, where in 1938, it reopened as "China City," described by Leonard and Dale Pitt, in *Los Angeles A to Z*, as "a block-long reconstruction of a street in China—as imagined by Hollywood." It is the story of Olvera Street, the "Mexican" marketplace built on the site of the original Los Angeles Plaza, which purports to offer an authentic taste of the old pueblo, although it was actually reconstructed in 1930 as a tourist site. Illusions all of them, fakes, replicas ... except that now they have become a part of L.A.'s history as well. 1930 was a long time ago, on the distant edge of living memory, which means the simulacrum has its own inherent value, that it tells us something about where and how we live. I think about this every time I wander down the eastern slope of Bunker Hill, on those steps adjacent to the raised railbed of Angels Flight, holding my breath as I sidestep puddles of urine, looking over to the concrete stanchions that support the two cars, Olivet and Sinai, of that ghostly railroad, locked in the stillness of entropy. This is the part of the walk my students hate, and to be honest, I'm not fond of it either, although it also tells us something about who uses this space, about the ways humanity and landscape intersect.

At the bottom of the stairs, I emerge onto Hill Street, once known as Calle de Toros, or Street of the Bulls. Then, I cross to Grand Central Market, since 1917 Los Angeles's largest public market, a cacophony of lunch counters and produce stalls. Originally developed to serve the professionals who lived on Bunker Hill (hence its proximity to Angels Flight), it has become, over

the last century, increasingly Latino, not unlike much of downtown itself. On the other side of the Market is Broadway, once
Eternity Street, now site of the most significant *mercado* in L.A.
And yet, this too, is changing, as all around us, different eras of
the city overlap. Over the last few years, Grand Central Market
has been upscaled, gentrified. In 2012, plans were announced to
bring in new vendors, keyed to a younger, more affluent consti-
tuency—the residential population of the Central City area,
which has risen, the *Los Angeles Times* has reported, "from an
estimated 18,652 residents in 1998 to nearly 50,000, according to
the Los Angeles Downtown Business Improvement District." Of
course, it was ever thus. Grand Central Market occupies the site
of the old Ville de Paris, which was, at a moment before any of
us were breathing, the city's finest department store, while the
building is a nineteenth-century landmark: Southern California's first steel-reinforced construction, erected in 1896. In the
early 1990s, during the second wave of downtown redevelopment, Ira Yellin restored it and the adjacent Million Dollar Theater, reconfiguring the upper floors of the complex, where Frank
Lloyd Wright worked in the 1920s, as residential space. For a
couple of years, a friend of mine lived above the Market, in a
condo that had once been William Mulholland's office; at night,
she said, she could smell cigar smoke, hear the low murmur of
conversation, and sometimes, if she were sleeping, feel the
weight of people sitting on the bed. When I asked what it was,
she said the place was haunted by the ghosts of the St. Francis
Dam disaster, in which hundreds (thousands, maybe) perished
after a dam Mulholland designed in the Santa Clara Valley
failed, flooding Castaic, Fillmore, and Santa Paula before reach-
ing the Pacific near Ventura. This effectively ended his domin-
ion over the Bureau of Water Works and Supply, and in its wake,

he went into seclusion. There is, however, something wild and vivid about the notion that three quarters of a century later, the specters of his avarice his negligence, might still come around to bother him for recompense.

Or, at least, there is to me. I love this story as much as any story I can tell about Los Angeles, love it because I don't know whether or not to believe it, even though I do not doubt my friend. I love its whiff of mystery, of spirit, love how it plays with (or against) one of the city's most prevalent creation myths, the promise *(There it is. Take it.)* that Mulholland improvised four years before Grand Central Market opened, as the water of the Owens River Valley began to cascade through the pebbled concrete channel of the first Los Angeles Aqueduct in the Newhall Pass. The history of L.A. is encoded in such a moment, a history of rapacious capitalism and vast infrastructure projects, of the men—and they were *all* men—who by their influence over various institutions (the *Times,* the Bureau of Water Works and Supply, the Pacific Electric Railway) used public resources for private good, building the city in the image of their greed. "From an airplane," Morrow Mayo noted in 1933, "Los Angeles today resembles half a hundred Middle-Western-Egyptian-English-Spanish communities, repainted and sprinkled about. Its population is about 1,4000,000. It is, and has been for ten years, the largest city in America in area, and people often wonder why. The answer is Water." This was Mulholland's dream, although it also illustrates how the city pushed beyond itself, expanding its nineteenth-century boundaries to embrace the sprawling distances we navigate today. "With abundant water on its way via the Los Angeles Aqueduct, smaller entities lined up to join the big city. Colegrove/Hollywood/East Hollywood came on board in 1910, and after 1913, big chunks of land expanded the city dramatically: the huge, 169-square-mile San Fernando addition opened up the Valley in 1915, and Westgate brought in 48 square miles of West L.A. in 1916," Glen Creason, map librarian of the Los Angeles Public Library, wrote in 2013 for the website of *Los Angeles* magazine. This part of the drama is familiar; indeed, it is rooted into Los Angeles's image of itself. The intersection of money, real estate, and technology: as early as 1917, it inspired Mary Austin's novel *The Ford* (although she changed the setting to Northern California), and later would infuse Cedric Belfrage's 1939 novel *Promised Land* and Robert Towne's 1974 movie *Chinatown.* No need here to spend time falling down that particular rabbit hole, except to point out that it was in Mulholland's office, at this very intersection in downtown L.A., that the entire narrative was dreamt up, bought, and paid for, which is why the ghosts meander back to exact their price.

The point, perhaps, is that stories ground us, even (or especially) when their currency remains in doubt. They offer a depth, a context, which becomes particularly important in a city built around a faith in reinvention, where the sun and lack of shadow—in addition to what we might refer to as a pervasive cultural mythology—lull us into imagining that we exist in a never-ending present tense. "I miss seasons," the director Peter Bogdonovich once said to Lawrence Weschler about Los Angeles, "and I hate the way the light of the place throws you into such a trance that you fail to realize how time is passing." He goes on to quote Orson Welles: "The terrible thing about L.A. is that you sit down, you're twenty-five, and when you get up you're sixty-two." I know just what they mean. I think of Raymond Chandler in *The Little Sister:* "I smelled Los Angeles before I got to it. It smelled stale and old like a living room that had been closed too long. But the colored lights fooled you. The lights were wonderful. There ought to be a monument to the man who invented neon lights. Fifteen stories high, solid marble. There's a boy who really made something out of nothing." It is this I used to resist the most after I first moved to Southern California, the oppressive midday glare in which the buildings bleach white against the pavement, reflecting nothing except the starkness of the semi-desert on which the city stands. I remember, during my first few months here, staring at billboards, storefronts, apartment buildings, thinking how ephemeral they all looked. Even the streets, laid down in what appeared to be large, individual slabs of asphalt, seemed as if they could come apart at the merest touch. Not knowing the place, I misread it, thinking it suggested something about transience. Now, I understand I was mistaken, that what I was seeing was, on the most basic level, a trick of the light.

Part of what brought me to such a reckoning was walking; if nothing else, it slowed my pace. I could make connections, or fail to make connections, could assess the city on my own terms, contemplate how my impressions (such as they were) did, or did not, cohere. I could speak a language in which I was fluent—that of the sidewalk, of the walker in the city—and apply it to a territory written in a different tongue. I could start to find a place, a narrative, to peel back the surfaces by which Los Angeles too often allowed itself to be defined. "Mysterious there prowl at the walker's heel," writes Robert Walser in his novella *The Walk*, "all kinds of thoughts and notions, such as make him stand in his ardent and regardless tracks and listen, because, again and again confused by curious impressions, by spirit power, he suddenly has the bewitching feeling that he is sinking into the earth, for an abyss has opened before the dazzled eyes of the thinker and the poet. His head wants to fall off. His otherwise so lively arms and legs are as benumbed. Countryside and people, sounds and colors, faces and farms, clouds and sunlight swirl all around him like diagrams; he asks himself: 'Where am I?'"

Where was I indeed? The answer I liked best was that I had come to the end of the line, the place where the myths of possibility and reinvention butt up against the edges of the continent, and the vanishing point of the horizon becomes the vanishing point of the known world. Another fantasy, another dream, this sunshine/noir dialectic, flip side of the cult of reinvention, which I never in any case believed. Maybe it was true one hundred years ago, or one hundred fifty, when you left your family on the East Coast, in Japan, or Europe, or Mexico, and never saw them again, living thousands of miles from home, across inhospitable, dangerous terrain. Even in New York, we learned about the Donner Party, but that was just a story now. By 1869, the transcontinental railroad had been completed; seven years later, a spur line to Southern California was in place. Little more than a decade after that, the "completion of the Santa Fe line," as Carey McWilliams observes in *Southern California Country: An Island on the Land*, effectively changed everything, leading to a rate war in which fares dropped to a dollar per ticket, "precipitat[ing] such a flow of migration, such an avalanche rushing madly to Southern California as I believe has no parallel." This is another of the region's essential creation myths, although unlike the one about the water, it undercuts itself. Cheap fares, abundant access ("In 1887," McWilliams tells us, "the Southern Pacific transported 120,000 people to Los Angeles, while the Santa Fe brought three and four passenger trains a day into the city") ... what we are seeing is the demystification of distance, the collapse of far away. "West of the west," Theodore Roosevelt famously labeled California, and he was right, in terms of mores, social vision, population, culture, style. Still, at the heart of such an assessment remains this fact: California had become available, which meant that people could come and go with ease. A hundred-plus years later, that's only more the case; during my first decade in California, I went east several times a year. Los Angeles, then, is no longer distant or exotic—no longer *exceptional*, as it were. "And surely we no longer can afford to erase our home out of forgetfulness, or worse, a willful amnesia," D.J. Waldie argued in 2000, "and imagine, as many want to, that we live in a historyless city, a placeless region, a Los Angeles devoid of contrarian surprises, an L.A. devoid of us and our sacred ordinariness."

Such sacred ordinariness implies a sense of what has come before, which is one of the stories downtown tells. It is readable in the line of the streets, the quick passage from Bunker Hill through Grand Central Market and out to Broadway, where the Bradbury building serves as both landmark and commercial space. This is it, the double vision, the layering that, increasingly, I see everywhere. When you look at the Bradbury, what do you imagine? I think of science fiction, which, to some extent, got its start right here. I think of Edgar Rice Burroughs and L. Frank Baum, writing in Tarzana and Hollywood in the decades after the railway wars, but even more, of the Los Angeles Science Fiction Society, which met at Seventh and Broadway, Clifton's Cafeteria, beginning in the 1930s, and counted among its members Ray Bradbury and Forrest J. Ackerman. Then, there is the Bradbury itself, the interior of which, the open corridors and iron latticework arranged around a skylit central atrium, was inspired by Edward Bellamy's 1887 utopian novel *Looking Backward*, science fiction before science fiction was invented, genre before it had a name. "It was the first interior of a twentieth century public building that I had ever beheld," Bellamy writes, "and the spectacle naturally impressed me deeply. I was in a vast hall full of light, received not alone from the windows on all sides, but from the dome, the point of which was a hundred feet above." The description fits the Bradbury to a T. What it suggests is that this is not just one of the last buildings of the nineteenth century but one of the first of the twentieth, and even, perhaps, of the twenty-first—all those ages, all those centuries, collapsing on top of one another—since it is also where the 1982 movie *Blade Runner* unfurls part of its dystopian vision of L.A. circa 2019, a city broken, shattered, disconnected and distinct from history.

By now, just a few years before the flashpoint it imagines, *Blade Runner* has grown dated, irrelevant, clichéd. Around that time, the downtown trolley is projected to be in operation, but even if that doesn't happen, there will be light rail from Santa Monica to Long Beach and Pasadena, and the Red Line expansion will be well underway. It is not, in other words, the world of *Blade Runner* we inherit, but more that of Norman Spinrad's 1987 rock-and-roll science fiction novel *Little Heroes*, in which characters travel by subway beneath the streets of the twenty-first-century city. Once again, back to the future, or back to the past, or forward to a place in which past and future blend together, and we can set aside the myths and the projections: Los Angeles as rootless, Los Angeles as fallen, a trope first imposed back in the 1880s, when Helen Hunt Jackson, like Bellamy a fantasist from Massachusetts, published her overwrought and sentimental novel *Ramona* and kicked off Southern California's mission craze. Jackson was a visitor, the first of many to try to read the city, although part of what she found here is astonishing in its consistency. "They seem to have been a variety of Centaur, these early Californian men," she explains in "Echoes in the City of Angels," published in a magazine called *The Century* in

1883. "They were seldom off their horses except to eat or sleep. They mounted, with jingling silver spur and glittering bridle, for the shortest distance, even to cross a plaza. They paid long visits on horseback, without ever dismounting. Clattering up to the window or door-sill, halting, throwing one knee over the crupper, the reins lying loose, they sat at ease, far more at ease than in a house." To walk in L.A., then—if, that is, we accept Jackson's account as both accurate and endemic—is to return to the beginning, to before the beginning, to reconceptualize the city as not just urban but also psychic space.

In recent years, of course, Los Angeles has begun to participate in such a process itself. Walk three blocks north and east from the Bradbury and you'll find evidence: the former Cathedral of St. Vibiana, built in 1876 on the corner of what is now Main and Second, catty-corner to the new police headquarters and a block from the *Los Angeles Times*. It's a building that predates nearly everything in the city, one that, red-tagged after the Northridge earthquake, has since been renovated and reopened as high-end event space. You don't need to be an Angeleno to appreciate the irony—consecrated ground reconfigured as a place of spectacle, the moneylenders in the temple, as we always knew they would be in the end. And yet, why not? L.A. has long been a city where faith and money wash each other's hands. "Here is the world's prize collection of cranks, semi-cranks, placid creatures whose bovine expression shows that each of them is studying, without much hope of success, to be a high-grade moron, angry or ecstatic exponents of food fads, sun-bathing, ancient Greek costumes, diaphragm breathing and the imminent second coming of Christ," Bruce Bliven wrote in *The New Republic* in 1927. This remains a resonant passage, though it oversimplifies. It was in Los Angeles that Sister Aimee Semple McPherson made herself a superstar, dedicating her Angelus Temple (it's still in use, in Echo Park), with its vaulted dome and five thousand-plus seats, on New Year's Day, 1923. It was in Los Angeles that Billy Graham became, in the realest sense imaginable, Billy Graham, spending eight weeks in the fall of 1949 preaching in a series of revival meetings that drew more than three hundred thousand followers to a circus tent erected at the corner of Hill Street and Washington Boulevard. "From 1850 to 1870," Carey McWilliams grumbled in 1940, "Los Angeles was 'the toughest town in the nation,' but it became the most priggish community in America after 1900. A glacial dullness engulfed the region. Every consideration was subordinated to the paramount concern of attracting church-going Middle Westerners to Southern California." There's more to the story, but McWilliams, in his fashion, nails it, tracing another creation myth that lingers just below the level of the street.

McPherson played a significant part in this, although she is largely forgotten today. In her moment—which began before her arrival in Los Angeles in 1918 and ended, effectively, on May 18, 1926, when she faked her own kidnapping and disappeared for five weeks in the company of the Angelus Temple's former radio operator, Kenneth Ormiston, a married man with whom she was having an affair—she was among America's highest profile personalities, comparable in visibility to Charles Lindbergh, Jack Dempsey, Babe Ruth. H.L. Mencken, no lover of Southern California, reported on her trial for obstruction of justice: "The Rev. sister in God, I confess," he mock-lamented, "greatly disappointed me." She appears, in one guise or another, in a slew of novels from the 1920s and 1930s: Upton Sinclair's *Oil!*, Sinclair Lewis's *Elmer Gantry*, Evelyn Waugh's *Vile Bodies*, Nathanael West's *The Day of the Locust*, Aldous Huxley's *After Many a Summer Dies the Swan*. In his magnificent *The Flutter of an Eyelid*, Myron

Brinig uses a sex-crazed McPherson stand-in named Angela Flower to embody L.A.'s desolate hypocrisy. (Among her proclamations? "Jesus is even in the scotch.") All this makes her, in many ways, a quintessential figure in the Los Angeles of her era, a city, in Huxley's pointed formulation, "of dreadful joy."

At the same time, when it comes to McPherson (and to Southern California itself), "there are more things in heaven and earth … than are dreamt of in your philosophy." For proof, we need look no further than her connection to another subterranean piece of L.A. history, the Asuza Street Revival that began in April 1906 and went on for nearly a decade; it was from the revival's dispersed faithful that she began to build a congregation of her own. This is ground zero for global Pentecostalism, right here in Little Tokyo, in a tiny dogleg stretch that extends for barely two blocks, from San Pedro Street around to Second. On the San Pedro side, there is a small historical marker: "Cradle of the Worldwide Pentecostal Movement." But this, too, is overlooked, forgotten … or more accurately, disregarded, since, for many of us, it's as if it were never there. How does that happen? How does a city obliterate, or ignore, its past? Again, it has to do with walking, or the lack of walking, the inability to still our gaze. In *The History of Forgetting*, Norman Klein cites Walter Benjamin: "In certain cities I noticed a real atrophy of the sidewalk. In Los Angeles, for example, on La Cienega, which is lined with bars, theaters, restaurants, antique dealers and private residences, the sidewalks are scarcely more than side-streets that lead customers and guests from the roadway into the house. Lawns have been planted from the façades to the roadway of this luxurious avenue. I followed a narrow path between the lawns for a time without meeting a living soul, while to my right, cars streamed by on the road; all animation in the street had taken refuge on the high road."

If that is true of a major thoroughfare such as La Cienega—and it *still* is; just a few weeks ago, I walked home from the Expo Line at La Cienega and Jefferson, thirty-five minutes through the industrial flats of Mid-City, radio stations and big box stores and party rental places and barely another pedestrian within sight—what then, of the intersection of Asuza and San Pedro, which is not even an intersection in any real sense, just the mouth of an alley in which something important happened in a different century? How can it be more than just another misbegotten reminder, relic of a historyless history? This is what I ask my students when we end our walk here, at the corner of San Pedro and Asuza, of the present and the past. Evangelism remains big in Southern California, although its center is now Orange County, and a neon "Jesus Saves" sign still lights up the night sky over downtown, a last vestige of the old Bible Institute of Los Angeles (reinvented as Biola University in La Mirada), founded in 1908 by Lyman Stewart, who also founded Union Oil. I don't know what it means, this confluence of God and fossil fuel; clearer to me is the hipster irony of that "Jesus Saves" sign blazing out across the city from the roof of the newly renovated United Artists Theatre building on Spring Street, which now houses the Ace Hotel. In a postmodern world, everything is up for grabs and all periods, all eons, blur. The never-ending present tense again, that curse and blessing of Los Angeles, enhanced by our reliance on the car. And will this change, has it already, with the rise of public transit and bike corridors? Or is it just another pitch, another come on, another instance of the boosterism for which L.A. has also long been known?

In the end, perhaps, it makes no difference. In the end, perhaps, we have no choice. Part of what we see in downtown now is the assertion, or the reassertion, of community, a function of terminal gridlock, if nothing else. Spring Street, the downtown trolley, the arts district—all reconfigurings of urban space—this is not *Blade Runner*, but *Back to the Future*, the story of a city looking through a convex mirror, reinventing itself in its own century-old image, which is an image we no longer recognize. Even L.A. Live, with its floodlights and LED screens, is a throwback to the days of Aldous Huxley: "On every building," he wrote in 1926, "the vertical lines of light went up like rockets into the dark sky. And the buildings themselves—they too had almost rocketed into existence. Thirty years ago Los Angeles was a one-horse—a half-horse—town. In 1940 or thereabouts it is scheduled to be as big as Paris. As big and as gay." Huxley meant that as a put-down—so much of the early literature of Southern California is the literature of put-down—and yet, almost nine decades later, it offers a reminder of both the city's hubris (note the use of that word "scheduled") and its limitations, of the history that, if we excavate it, opens up Los Angeles in unexpected ways.

There is a photograph I especially like, taken circa 1900, in the half-horse days Huxley pokes fun at, looking north on Spring past Third Street, the Douglas building in the middle distance, pavement dotted with horse-drawn carriages, bikes, and trolleys, sidewalks loosely clustered with pedestrians. This is the image of a city in its infancy, but that's not why it strikes me; rather, I am drawn by it as by a kind of living memory. As it happens, I am familiar with the Douglas building, or at least with the commercial space on the ground floor, which in the picture is protected from L.A.'s relentless sky and sunlight by a series of large striped awnings, of the sort that were then in common use. For a number of years, I used to drink there, in a sushi place called Origami; a couple of afternoons a week, I would walk down from the *Los Angeles Times*, where I was then an editor, in time for happy hour. I had no idea of the legacy of the building, except in the sense that it fulfilled, for me, one of the great benefits of urban living: a place to go, within walking distance of one's home or office, a neighborhood joint, a corner bar, a place where, even in the loosest sense, it might be said that you belong. Our experience of cities is built out of relationships such as this—informal, of the moment, unplanned and serendipitous ... organic in the most fundamental sense. Origami closed in 2011, but every time I walk by the Douglas, I am confronted by its residue. Memento mori, Norman Klein would argue, "an idealized face left over from childhood—a photograph, the color of mother's dress in the day she took ill (the photological trace)." Yes, and more than that, as well. "If we concentrate," he continues, "the imago seems to be waiting for us intact.... It remains where we put it, but the details around it get lost, as if they were haunted, somewhat contaminated, but empty." Is it a stretch to imagine that he might be talking about all of Los Angeles? Is it a stretch to suggest that this is the challenge of living in such a place? Memory and meaning, collective and personal experience, it all gets blurred together, or at least for me it does, leaving me to look for recognition where I find it: in the movement of my feet across urban sidewalks, where the story of the city reveals itself in ghostly traces, in the spaces we might never think to look.

"Did I ever tell you about the ugliest place in Los Angeles?" Klein once asked me, apropos of nothing.

> I decided it was in Van Nuys, at the intersection of Fulton and Burbank. I selected it because it wasn't poverty; it was just ugly, retinal eye burn of an extreme form. On one corner was a place called Father and Me, which repaired cars. It was surrounded by rolls of barbed wire like some old lady's hair. Across the street was a very

bad *trompe l'oeil* lumberyard that looked like it was going to fall over. Then, there was this strange Middle Eastern restaurant in a dumpy building with a faded image on top of a man holding a chicken. It was like that in every direction.

Eventually, Klein discovered that beneath this desolate veneer of blankness were overlapping populations of Lebanese and Palestinians and Israelis. A map of the Middle East emerged. "Little by little," he concluded, "this was not the ugliest place in Los Angeles, it was just the best erased example of urban complexity. And I thought, Wow, this is one crazy city to have that much happening with so little heat you can actually see."

Falling Down

They say L.A. is large, but they lie.
Carolyn See

I am a reluctant Angeleno. Even after all these years, nearly a quarter century. Or maybe reluctant is not the right word; maybe it's more a matter of ambivalence. Lifer again, not (never) a native, as if Los Angeles were some amorphous landscape of incarceration, and I were serving out a stretch of time. In *My Dinner with André*, André Gregory describes an encounter at Findhorn, the Scottish spiritual community. "And when I was at Findhorn," he tells his dinner companion, the skeptical Wallace Shawn,

> I met this extraordinary English tree expert.... He said to me, "Where are you from?" And I said, "New York." And he said, "Ah, New York, yes, that's a very interesting place. Do you know a lot of New Yorkers who keep talking about the fact that they want to leave, but never do?" And I said, "Oh, yes." And he said, "Why do you think they don't leave?" And I gave him different banal theories. And he said, "Oh, I don't think it's that way at all." He said, "I think that New York is the new model for the new concentration camp, where the camp has been built by the inmates themselves, and the inmates are the guards, and they have this pride in this

thing that they've built—they've built their own prison—and so they exist in a state of schizophrenia where they are both guards and prisoners. And as a result they no longer have—having been lobotomized—the capacity to leave the prison they've made or even to see it as a prison." And then he went into his pocket, and he took out a seed for a tree, and he said, "This is a pine tree." And he put it in my hand. And he said, "Escape before it's too late."

That's a telling bit of commentary, not least because, more than three decades later, Gregory still lives, at least part of the time, in New York. Equally important, it raises questions about how we imagine the cities in which we find ourselves, how we frame our discomforts, our dissatisfactions—and, I suppose, our pleasures also—through their lenses. When I lived in New York, I felt at times very much as Gregory's tree expert imagines: bound up, confined by the city, all its concrete corridors. I couldn't wait to leave, and yet, apparently, I could. It took several years of false starts and back-and-forths before I finally moved to California, where I had lived, briefly, as a child and then again at eighteen. Once I arrived, all I wanted was to go back home. I spent my first few months in Los Angeles lamenting the aimlessness of it, not the sprawl but the emptiness, an emptiness so diffuse, so disturbing, and (yes) so unexpected, that I didn't feel as if I were living in a city at all. That first summer (I arrived in May), I would wake in the mornings and feel the heat suffusing the trees outside my kitchen window like a kind of rising fever, sunlight thick and yellow as a smear of something, dust or mucus, in my eyes. I felt slow, mealy in my bones; time did not exist here, or did not exist in quite the way I was used to, as something pressing in on me. This would be a relief to some, but for me, it felt more like an illness, an infection, as if I'd given up my urgency. "Where else should they go but California, the land of sunshine and oranges?" Nathanael West writes in *The Day of the Locust*, evoking the end-of-the-road blankness that even by the late 1930s was already part of the personality of the place. "Once there, they discover that sunshine isn't enough. They get tired of oranges, even of avocado pears and passion fruit. Nothing happens. They don't know what to do with their time." More than half a century later, it seemed, nothing had changed. Days passed in a haze of light and lassitude. For all the time I had spent here, as a visitor, as a traveler, I did not, it turned out, know the city at all. It was like some strange sort of overbuilt suburban hybrid: *rurban*, in Carey McWilliams's well-wrought word. I joked, to myself mostly, with an edge of bitter irony, that I had moved to the country for the summer, but even that did not seem directionless enough. Where was I? Why had I come? Before leaving New York, I would have said I knew the answers to those questions, but now that I was here, I was no longer sure.

What I can tell you now is that this was a problem of translation. My wife and I had come west with a single car, and she was working; I was too, but in the neighborhood. In the cities I knew, the cities where I had lived, walking would have been a matter of reflex; I had only rarely driven in those cities anyway. Los Angeles, however, came loaded with its own specific (lack of) context clues. I don't want to say that L.A. doesn't have a logic, that it is sprawling, random, a city without narrative—although this is a story I have, at various times, embraced. Exceptionalism again, which is, of course, both true and false, although ultimately never true enough. At the same time, I think, the dichotomy is one reason why the city so bewilders so many of us, especially those who come from somewhere else. Read much of the critical commentary about the place—that it is shallow, that it lacks an intellectual or literary life, that it repels the very notion of community—and what you are confronting are the preconceptions of the observers, who have, most likely, parachuted in from other, more established locales. Architecture is a particular target, what Norman Mailer has described as "the endless repetitions of that city which is the capital of suburbia with its milky pinks, its washed-out oranges, its tainted lime yellows of pastel on one pretty little architectural monstrosity after another, the colors not intense enough, the styles never pure, and never sufficiently impure to collide on the eye." So too is the (apparent) inaccessibility of the street. Here's Mailer again: "Los Angeles is a city to drive in, the boulevards are wide, the traffic is nervous and fast, the radio stations play bouncing, blooping, rippling tunes, one digs the pop in a pop tune, no one of character would make love by it but the sound is good for swinging a car, electronic guitars and Hawaiian burps." Or Truman Capote, from his 1947 essay "Hollywood": "There is a sleight-of-hand about distance here, nothing is so near as you supposed, and it is not unusual to travel ten miles for a package of cigarettes." See what we're up against? I have never known anyone to travel ten miles for a pack of cigarettes, not ever, not even once, nor do I know what character has to do with making love. In "Hollywood," Capote also mocks the idea of spending Christmas in Southern California, where "tinsel, twinkling on twenty-four-karat sunshine, hangs everywhere like swamp moss." For him, Christmas is "out of place in Hollywood," because the weather tells him so. But what is the weather in Bethlehem in December? And what does that suggest about authenticity?

This is what all these years in L.A. have taught me, that the only strategy for reckoning with the place is to employ a kind of double vision, by which we peel back the clichés, the received wisdom *(received from whom?* I often wonder), and interact with the city on its terms. Yes, Los Angeles *is* sprawling, random, without narrative … except, of course, when it is not. Yes, it can be still and sun-baked, with, as Capote writes, "an air of Sunday vacancy; here where no one walks [and] cars glide in a constant shiny silent stream"—but the same, I'd argue, might be said of any city where someone shows up for a few days or a few weeks and tries to come to a conclusion, rather than to engage. "Los Angeles," John Gregory Dunne wrote in the 1970s, "is the least accessible and therefore the worst reported of American cities. It is not available to the walker in the city. There is no place where the natives gather. Distance obliterates unity and community. This inaccessibility means that the contemporary de Tocqueville on a layover between planes can define Los Angeles only in terms of his own culture shock."

Dunne is taking note of something defining about the landscape, but even more, he's critiquing the standards of the critique. For him, and for me also, it's more useful, or legitimate, to think of L.A. in terms of its smaller narratives … the city as collage, as mash-up, in which our personal experience becomes a way to adapt, to normalize, to make the streets accessible to us. If there's an underlying principle at work, it may be aporia, a Greek concept Norman Klein defines as a state of willful dissociation, a strategy for seeking, and finding, what we least expect. Such a narrative impulse reflects the notion we often have of L.A. as open-ended, inconclusive—a series of beginnings rather than any definitive end. As an example, consider how hard it is merely to define the place: as a state of being, that is, not a state of mind. What do we talk about when we talk about Los Angeles? Is it the city? Is it the county? And what of all those independent municipalities (Beverly Hills, Inglewood, West Hollywood, Santa Monica, Culver City) that exist surrounded on all sides by L.A., neither a part of it nor apart? "Seventy-two suburbs in search of a city," Dorothy Parker once quipped. The same, to be sure, is true of its history. Founded in 1781, it remains, for all intents and purposes, a twentieth-century dreamscape, reliant, in the most concrete terms imaginable, on the interplay of speed and light.

Here we see what walking offered: a way of keeping the city bounded, of making it small. To move to this place had been, for me, a kind of culture shock. I needed a mechanism to rewrite the landscape in terms I could understand. Only a few months after I arrived, I spent an afternoon with Carolyn See at her home in Topanga Canyon, where she presented a first glimpse of a psychic map of Los Angeles. I had already read her novel *Golden Days*, with its admonition about the "real" L.A., which "had its thick, coiled root downtown, and on the east, little underground rootlets; obscure Mexican restaurants. Then a thin stem, the Santa Monica freeway, heading due west and putting out greenery, places in this western desert where you'd love to live—if things went right." Such a vision appealed to me, with its whisper of Manhattan, another long and narrow corridor, bound on the southern side by the freeway and on the northern by the Hollywood Hills, stretching from downtown to the beach. I could visualize that, I could see it; it felt like something I could grasp. For See, however, this was only one way to think about the city and not even the most important—more essential was the role of private life. "In Southern California," she insisted, "you don't go down to the cafe and drink a lot of coffee and talk about intellectual concepts the way you might in Prague. You get in the car, drive for an hour, have a long, leisurely lunch in a beautiful yard, and get the same material covered. There's a kind of daytime quality to a lot of literary life here—not a suburban quality, but a domestic one." Such a vision echoes Louis Adamic, he of the enormous village, with his notion of Los Angeles as less metropolis than garden city, although for him, such a vision, anti-urban and, even worse, anti-intellectual, was one of the most distressing aspects of the place. "Los Angeles," he wrote in 1932, "grew up suddenly, *planlessly*, under the stimuli of the adventurous spirit of millions of people and the profit motive. It is still growing. Here everything has a chance to thrive—for a while—as a rule only a brief while. Inferior as well as superior plants and trees flourish for a time, then both succumb to chaos and decay."

I wanted to believe in See's optimism, but Adamic's cynicism kept getting in the way. I was working for an alt-weekly whose offices were a mile and a half from where I lived: south on Crescent Heights to Wilshire, then east on Wilshire, past the County Museum, the Tar Pits, along that corridor of office towers. A block one way was the Shanghai Winter Garden, a Chinese restaurant dating from the 1930s with a dim and mossy bar. I could almost imagine Philip Marlowe drinking there in the quiet darkness of a weekday afternoon. A block the other way was the El Rey Theatre, not yet renovated, to which Marlowe had once glancingly referred. I mention this only to suggest my ignorance, my nostalgia—if it is possible to have nostalgia for a city you don't know. This, too, is among the hallmarks of L.A., going back to its beginnings. "With the beginning of the prosperity of the City of the Angels," Helen Hunt Jackson wrote in the 1880s, "came the end of its primeval peace." Sixty-five years later, in *The Little Sister*, Marlowe plays his own variation on this theme. "I used to like this town," he growls, by way of Raymond Chandler.

A long time ago. There were trees along Wilshire Boulevard. Beverly Hills was a country town. Westwood was bare hills and lots offering at eleven hundred dollars and no takers. Hollywood was a bunch of frame houses on the interurban line. Los Angeles was just a big dry sunny place with ugly homes and no style, but good-hearted and peaceful. It had the climate they just yap about now. People used to sleep out on porches. Little groups who thought they were intellectual used to call it the Athens of America. It wasn't that, but it wasn't a neon-lighted slum either.

For me, the nostalgia was *for* that neon-lighted slum, noir city of the 1930s, corrupt and recognizable and bleak. I loved the idea of it—Southern California not as landscape of reinvention but rather as end of the line. This was the vision defined by Chandler, West, and Fante, with their dust- and smog-choked palm trees, their degradation and decay. It was a vision that marked L.A. as a lonely place, and since I was lonely, disconnected, that felt like the real Los Angeles to me. Take this walk, for example, which I made several times a week, back and forth from home to office, a walk that in a different sort of city would have been routine, mundane, unremarked and unremarkable, the most basic experience of urban life. Here, it was like passing through an alien landscape, unpopulated except for the landmarks ... not a film set (I rejected, then as now, that reading of the city) but something more like the elusive texture of a reverie.

In *Los Angeles: The Architecture of Four Ecologies*, Reyner Banham zeroes in on this stretch of Wilshire, known as Miracle Mile, a name coined, with typical boosterish hubris, in the 1920s by developer A. W. Ross. Banham calls it "the first real monument of the Motor Age," a western commercial hub built to compete with downtown. It's hard to imagine the looseness of those roots now, with Wilshire among the city's iconic boulevards, home to the nation's most densely traveled bus line, a spine that, like

See's "thin stem" of freeway, extends from downtown to the beach. Yet as recently as the early 1920s—still, perhaps barely, within living memory—the area was essentially unpopulated, empty but for a pair of airfields, one owned by Cecil B. De Mille and the other by Charlie Chaplin's brother Syd, across the street from each other at the intersection of Wilshire and Fairfax Avenue. There is a photograph, taken in 1920, looking east along Wilshire: in the middle distance, oil wells pock the grounds of what will later be the County Museum. We see no buildings, no sidewalks, just a ribbon of macadam, a ghost whisper of what is to come. According to Banham, Ross had already identified the boulevard's commercial potential; the idea was to serve "the probable shopping habits of the new, affluent, and motorized inhabitants of areas like Beverly Hills, the westerly parts of Hollywood, or the areas of the Wolfskill Ranch that were about to become Westwood and Holmby Hills." Within a decade, Miracle Mile was transformed into what Banham calls "the first linear downtown," its shops "hard up to the sidewalk so that it looks like a conventional shopping street," but with "parking-lots at the rear." The result is a peculiar variant on urbanity, made more so by the "residential areas immediately behind the parking-lots and almost seventy thousand souls within walking distance." Like so much in L.A., these innovations had less to do with planning than with politics. "Downtown interests," Banham notes, worried over competition, insisted Wilshire be zoned as "a broad residential avenue.... Ross therefore had to negotiate or litigate a 'spot' waiver to the residential zoning for every site, and this he could only do for substantial and well-regarded clients." It didn't matter. The development of Wilshire Boulevard is as significant, in its way, as the building of the aqueduct, as essential to the creation of contemporary Los

Angeles. We can lament the source, the motivation, see it as an expression of money looking after money, but the effect, which is the evolution of a decentered city, is the same. "The point," Banham concludes, "about this giant city, which has grown almost simultaneously all over, is that all its parts are equal and equally accessible from all other parts at once."

That this is no longer even remotely true goes without saying; the fluidly automotive city Banham celebrated has become the stuff of wishful fantasy. Still, the ideal lingers: a city that grows out, not up, that is only now reckoning with the restrictions of geography that New York and San Francisco, among other cities, have long since had to face. A generation ago, in *City of Quartz*, Mike Davis lamented the amorphous, sprawling metastasis of a megalopolis without limitation. The "Los Angeles of the next millennium," he called it, "stretching ... from the country-club homes of Santa Barbara to the shanty *colonias* of Ensenada, to the edge of Llano in the high desert," where phantom communities were mapped and platted in some bizarre recreation of the real estate boom a century before. Now, that image seems nothing if not obsolete, a vision rooted wholly in the past. Instead, L.A. has begun to contract, to turn back on itself, aware that sprawl can only go so far. "The prototypical suburban context of the city," architect Michael Maltzan writes in *No More Play: Conversations on Urban Speculation in Los Angeles and Beyond*, "has given way to an emerging context of real physical intensity and population density. The indicators are visible. Higher levels of new infill buildings and projects are being developed. Large masses of buildings form suddenly in empty lots. Easy mobility decreases as the freeways turn into virtual gridlock well before and well after the traditional rush-hour expectations. Mass transit hubs have emerged.... Now the bounding perimeter of the city has been hit, and perceptual, psychological, and physical limits of what it means to be in Los Angeles have arrived."

What does this mean to the pedestrian? For me, it provokes an uneasy dislocation between L.A. as it is and as it claims to be. Walking in this city comes with its own odd edge of drift, of *dérive*. Partly, it's because we know we shouldn't be here; edenic myths aside, Southern California is an unforgiving place. Water again (of which there is never enough, especially now in the midst of a drought acknowledged as the worst in California history), but also earthquakes, fires, Santa Ana winds. "It is hard for people who have not lived in Los Angeles," Joan Didion observes in her 1968 essay "Los Angeles Notebook,"

> to realize how radically the Santa Ana figures in the local imagination. The city burning is Los Angeles's deepest image of itself: Nathanael West perceived that, in *The Day of the Locust*; and at the time of the 1965 Watts riots what struck the imagination most indelibly were the fires.... Los Angeles weather is the weather of catastrophe, of apocalypse, and, just as the reliably long and bitter winters of New England determine the way life is loved there, so the violence and the unpredictability of the Santa Ana affect the entire quality of life in Los Angeles, accentuate its impermanence, its unreliability. The wind shows us how close to the edge we are.

With that as a collective context, is it any wonder we bring a certain anxiety to our thinking about Los Angeles, a city that did not so much develop as impose itself upon the landscape, like a map of someplace else? Aporia again, a three-dimensional expression of the Situationist ideal, which forces us to be present by seeing the terrain through a different set of eyes. L.A. encodes such a demand even when it doesn't know what it is doing, which is to say: *every day*. Where else would the simple act of walking be so loaded, a source of pride and policy as much as comedy and cliché? I think, once more, of Walter Benjamin, who in 1933 argued that "Nature produces similarities; one need only think of mimicry. The highest capacity for producing similarities, however, is man's." What Benjamin was getting at, the architect Neil Leach elaborates, is "the theory of *mimesis*," which offers, in this usage anyhow, "a way of finding meaning in the world through a discovery of similarities." In his 2006 book *Camouflage*, Leach applies such a filter to the full array of urban interactions, seeing it as a mechanism of assimilation or adaptation, made essential by our alienation from the world in which we live. Benjamin again: "The twentieth century, with its porosity and transparency, its tendency toward the well-lit and airy, has put an end to dwelling in the old sense." That is exactly how I felt—and, to some extent, still feel—about Los Angeles. It is why, when I arrived, I did everything I could to reimagine the city, to re-walk it, in my own image, or at least in the image of other cities where I'd lived. My first month here, I attended a neighborhood association meeting, the earliest indication I had that in this never-ending grid of streets and sidewalks, the notion of the neighborhood might somehow be in play. The point of the meeting, though, was not community, at least not as I defined it, but its opposite—to stand against plans for a subway that would run the length of Wilshire Boulevard. This was a year and a half before the Red Line opened, its first leg a four-plus mile run from Union Station to MacArthur Park ... less subway as transport network than as some sort of abstract idea. At the meeting, I objected to the community's objections, seeing them as short-sighted, retrograde. There was some good- (and not so good-) natured back and forth, then someone asked, "You're not really saying you want a subway station in the neighborhood?"

I looked at him, not understanding the issue. "In the neigh-borhood?" I answered. "I want a subway station on my block."

On the one hand, this represents a case of culture shock or cul-ture clash, evidence of an unbridgeable divide. It's what Angele-nos hate about New Yorkers: the endless comparisons, the value judgments, the insistence on Manhattan as urban ideal. At the same time, I want to say, I wasn't wrong. Consider Maltzan's "per-ceptual, psychological and physical limits," to which certain long-term L.A. residents find themselves unable to adapt. Not long ago, I was in an accident in Pasadena; for two weeks, my car was in the shop. Rather than the rental route, I went Metro—mostly on the Expo Line, which extends from Culver City to downtown. It was not a New York experience, but one indigenous to Los Angeles. I was often driven to the train, as if I were a suburban (or at least *rurban*) commuter; the city I crossed—at street level—was the one with which I've had to come to terms: diffuse, resistant to pedestrians. At the same time, I felt a whisper of what L.A. may be growing into, now that it can no longer continue growing out. I felt, in other words, a sense of density, of destiny, of the city it will necessarily become. I hesitate to write that because of how much I loathe this way of thinking; it is the very worst thing about Los Angeles, the hype and hucksterism, the (yes) exceptionalism. God forbid I should sound like Mark Lee Luther, whose 1924 novel *The Boosters* breathlessly assures us, "You can't beat Southern Califor-nia. It's the garden spot of the globe and Los Angeles is the pick of the garden." This is the rhetoric James M. Cain mocked in his 1933 essay "Paradise" (promoted on the cover of H. L. Mencken's *Amer-ican Mercury* under the banner "What Southern California Is Really Like"): "Where this place is headed is to be the leader in commerce, art, citrus production, music, rabbit breeding, oil pro-duction, furniture manufacture, walnut growing, literature, olive bottling, short- and long-distance hauling, clay modeling, aesthetic criticism, fish export, canary-bird culture, playwrighting, shipping, cinematic creativeness, and drawing-room manners. In short, it is going to be a paradise on earth." And yet, even Cain, cynical as he was, couldn't help concluding that "with such vaulting ambitions, it might pull off something: you can't tell. It is keenly aware of the Orient, and also of Mexico; streams are meeting here that ought to churn up some exciting whirlpools. I, personally, even if the first act hasn't been so hot, am not going to walk out on the show."

The truth, of course, is that it doesn't matter, that for better or worse, this is the city in which we are. That's true whether we're talking about the get-richer-quick schemes that brought irrigation to the Valley, or the commercial interests that developed Wilshire Boulevard. We miss the point by comparing, by framing Los Angeles as somehow larger, smaller, wilder, or more catastrophic than life. We overlook the reality in favor of the mythos, which is (don't get me wrong) compelling, but also fundamentally beside the point. How do we engage with the city as an actual place, with actual people and actual problems, when it remains, even for those of us who live here, tempting to read as metaphor? How do we deconstruct the stories, all the dreams and dramas, and allow ourselves instead to see it plain? Partly, I think, the answer is to do what Cain did, to approach the city through Keats's negative capability, which requires that we balance two opposing ideas in our heads at the same time. "Of course," Gregory Rodriguez wrote in a 2009 *Los Angeles Times* column about the Station fire, which burned 160,000 acres in the Angeles National Forest over a period of three weeks that autumn, "competing images of California—and particularly Los Angeles—as heaven or hell are a well-trodden cliché." Faced with the beauty of the fire's residue, especially the "pyrocumulus clouds" that mushroomed over the Los Angeles basin like atomic fallout, he found a new way to define the terms. "Far from being the victory of hell in L.A. over heaven in L.A.," Rodriguez continued, "[those clouds] reminded me that in a very real way, we can't have one without the other. The cloud is just what it looked like: two sides of the same coin; the one defines the other. Heaven, hell. Ugly, beautiful. Apocalypse, paradise. Los Angeles."

Heaven, hell. Ugly, beautiful. Apocalypse, paradise. Yes, I think: that's it. In the movie *Falling Down*, Michael Douglas plays a character named William Foster, who embodies, wittingly or otherwise, this dichotomy. Known as D-FENS because of his vanity license plate, Foster has been laid off from his defense industry job; as the action opens, he abandons his beater car in standstill traffic near the 110–101 connector and literally descends, down the slope of a freeway embankment, into the inferno, a city on the verge of combustion from heat and overload. Over the course of one long afternoon, Foster walks from downtown to Venice (another variation on See's "thin stem"), navigating the archipelagos of a divided urban landscape, confronting gangbangers, neo-Nazis, wealthy duffers, the faceless complacency of the corporate state. His is a peculiarly identifiable breaking point: the instant the petty indignities and degradations of contemporary culture become too much. And yet, Foster—or, for that matter, the film itself—is no archetype, but rather the reflection of a particular moment in L.A.'s life.

Released in February 1993, *Falling Down* was shot on streets that, before filming was completed, would erupt in rioting when four Los Angeles police officers were acquitted for the beating of Rodney King. The tensions the film highlights, then, are as specific to their time as a news photograph. So, too, the reactionary aspects of the narrative, which portrays, among other things, a white man on the outs. "I'm the bad guy?" Foster asks late in the movie, just seconds before the inevitable denouement. "How'd that happen? I did everything they told me to. Did you know I build missiles? ... I helped to protect America. You should be rewarded for that. But instead they give it to the plastic surgeons. You know they lied to me." There's a whisper of class-consciousness at work here, although a character such as Foster would never allow himself to see that, to recognize that the deck has been stacked by the very power structure he's worked his professional life to preserve. Rather, it is left to the cop who has pursued him, a desk sergeant, played by Robert Duvall, on his last day before retirement, to deliver the final message. "Is that what this is about?" he asks, referring to the swath of mayhem Foster has cut across the city. "You're angry because you got lied to? ... Hey, they lie to everyone. They lie to the fish. But that doesn't give you any special right to do what you did today."

I've long had a soft spot for *Falling Down;* it is a touchstone film to me because of what it says about Los Angeles—on the surface and between the lines. The Southern California it portrays is very much the one eulogized on the January 31, 1994 cover of *Time* magazine: "The latest catastrophe in a string of disasters," the teaser copy warns, "rocks the state to the core, forcing Californians to ponder their fate and the fading luster of its golden dream." The catastrophe in question, of course, was the 6.7 Northridge earthquake, which broke along a previously unmapped fault in the San Fernando Valley at 4:31 A.M. on January 17, 1994—the midpoint in a four-year string of disruptions and upheavals, both natural and civil, beginning with the beating of Rodney King and ending with the O.J. Simpson trial. That all this coincided roughly with my relocation to L.A. is a coincidence on which I don't especially choose to dwell, except to say it made me feel at home. In contrast with the silence and diffusion of my first months in the city, the mix of riots, wild-fires, floods, and earthquakes taught me that there was more at work here than met the eye. These sprawling distances, these boulevards and mini-malls and overpasses—all of it masked a territory far more elemental, where beneath the stillness lurked chaos, which bubbled over everywhere. Later, I would recognize the antecedents: the Rodney King riots were not just a reaction to the acquittal of four white cops by an all-white jury in the videotaped beating of a black man, but also the expression of a lineage, a heritage of discrimination, going back to the 1965 Watts riots, to the 1943 Zoot Suit riots, to housing covenants and miscegenation laws, to the Mexican-American War. History again, and how it plays out across generations, even (or especially) if we remain unaware. Darryl Gates, the police chief who let South Los Angeles burn for hours on the first night of the riots while he attended a political fundraiser, a man notorious for saying that African American suspects died from chokeholds because their arteries "do not open up as fast as normal people," learned his particular brand of racial politics at the hand of an earlier police chief, William Parker, who was himself decried for fueling tensions between whites, blacks, and Latinos in the years leading up to Watts.

Here, we find another argument against exceptionalism, the seductive mythos of the promised land. What *Falling Down* portrays, perhaps unintentionally, is the moment the old Los Angeles gets put to rest. It is the psychic precursor of the May Day 2006 immigration rallies, in which something like two million protestors gridlocked downtown, and in the process reclaimed the city's streets as public space. It is a portrait of the crucible from which the new L.A., the one we have begun to occupy, is forged. It's no coincidence that even as William Foster trekked his fictional way across the basin, that contested Red Line subway was under construction; the first leg, from Union Station to MacArthur Park, opened on January 30, 1993, a month before the film's release. At the time, that didn't seem like much, but it has turned out to be a development as necessary, as revolutionary, as the building of the Arroyo Parkway. Within seven years, the Red Line would extend beyond its initial five-station loop, underneath the Cahuenga Pass to Universal City, where in a stunning bit of irony, the platform features a public art installation commemorating the treaty signed at Campo de Cahuenga in 1847, by General Pio Pico and John C. Frémont, ending hostilities between Mexico and the United States. This is one of the most significant events in California history, as much an origin story as the 1906 earthquake or the completion of the transcontinental railroad, but it exists for us almost entirely beneath conscious reckoning. Sprawl, containment, randomness, serendipity: it all adds up to a story in which context eludes us ... except that context is everywhere, if we know how to see.

In a 2014 piece in *The New Yorker*, Adam Gopnick quotes the French philosopher Frédéric Gros: "Walking is *not* a sport." William Foster would agree with that, and so, in many ways, do I. Gros, Gopnick explains, breaks walking into three categories: contemplative, "cynical" (in the sense of "the Cynics of ancient Greece, homeless hippies who scorned conventions, customs, clothes"), and what we have come to think of (thanks to our old friend Walter Benjamin, by way of Baudelaire) as that of the *flâneur*. To this, I would add a fourth classification, the walk as mechanism of narrative, of liberation even, a way to find and maintain one's place. That liberation can be a matter of social hierarchies: think of Foster, traversing a cross-section of the city's neighborhoods, challenged by gangsters and golfers alike. This is how we're taught to think about Los Angeles, as a divided city, in which self-interest and isolation trump any notion of the greater good. But let me propose an alternative, in which walking roots us, connecting us both to the city as it is, and also to its history. About halfway through *Falling Down*, Foster finds himself in Miracle Mile, at the same intersection, Wilshire and Detroit, where Mary Louise Parker gets robbed in *Grand Canyon*. In part, I suppose, both scenes were shot along this stretch— the films came out two years apart—because it is so recognizably urban, Banham's horizontal downtown in present tense; in another part, because it evokes a vision of the city that these movies share. I, however, am drawn by something else, a little detail, the kind (perhaps) only a pedestrian would recognize. As Foster wanders Wilshire, he passes the Sher-E Punjab, an Indian restaurant that was once The Darkroom, a camera shop. This storefront may be my favorite L.A. landmark, what the Los Angeles Conservancy calls "one of the city's last remaining examples of programmatic architecture, in which a building resembles its purpose." Built in 1938, it features a black vitriolite façade in the shape of an Argus camera, with lens, shutter, f-stops, flash. It's a throwback to restaurants that look like hot dogs or derbies, to the architecture derided by Mailer and Capote, to what Nathanael West, in the opening pages of *The Day of the Locust*, dismisses as a new form of grotesque. "Few things are sadder than the truly monstrous," West writes, dismissing "the Mexican ranch houses, Samoan huts, Mediterranean villas, Egyptian and Japanese temples, Swiss chalets, Tudor cottages," the indulgences of a city with no propriety or style.

"On the corner of La Huerta Road," he continues, "was a minia-
ture Rhine castle with tarpaper turrets pierced by archers. Next
to it was a highly colored shack with domes and minarets out of
the *Arabian Nights*.... Both houses were comic, but he didn't
laugh. Their desire to startle was so eager and guileless."

The same might be said of The Darkroom, which, I should
point out, is no longer an Indian restaurant. Another iteration,
another adaptation, another example of how the city changes,
even when it doesn't change so very much. And yet, like the
Douglas building downtown, it also roots me—and not just
because I used to go there, not infrequently, for lunch. This is
my neighborhood, broadly speaking, the one in which I've lived
since I first moved here and began to walk this boulevard as if it
might tell me something about where I was. Even after all these
years, nearly a quarter century, I think of it as a lodestone, a
compass point. There is a photograph, preserved in the Los
Angeles City Archive, of Olympic Boulevard looking east from
Fairfax, just a mile or so from here, taken in 1931. That's seven
years before The Darkroom opened, a decade past DeMille and
Chaplin's air fields, two or three years after the invention of
Miracle Mile. Today, the intersection is among the most chaotic
in the city: three major streets, Olympic, Fairfax, and San
Vicente, coming together in a vortex. In 1931, though, there is
nothing: just some telephone poles and a railroad crossing sign,
a couple of buildings and three cars in the distance driving
towards downtown. When I posted the image on Facebook, a
friend commented that by the time he grew up in this neighborhood in the 1950s, everything had changed. "Between the time
this photo was taken and when my memories begin," he writes,
"this whole stretch of Olympic was built up with apartment

buildings, the Westside Jewish Community Center and the community hospital (Midway) where I had my tonsils removed. This area became the heart of Jewish L.A. The Ethiopian restaurants occupy spaces that once had Yiddish signs in the windows—bakeries, kosher restaurants, a kosher butcher, and Sammy's restaurant with 'Delicate-Essen' in green neon over the front window."

Needless to say, I don't remember any of that—it was before my time in every sense. But there is a temptation to read it as an expression of L.A.'s instability, its ephemerality, the evanescence even of established neighborhoods. The speed of development here, such a logic tells us, the creation of whole communities, vast swaths of urban territory in what is really no more than a generation, explains the rootlessness of the city, its perverse relationship with history. Such a story offers a variation on the theme of sunshine, that sense of the eternal present, the lightness with which the city lies upon the land. And yes, there is a touch of (let's call it) seismic existentialism here, the sense that in a landscape of constant physical upheaval, one that can, at any moment, literally erase itself, the only constant is the pace of change. It's a common story, one I once liked to tell myself, although I don't want to tell it anymore. There are two sides to every narrative, and the other side of this one exists outside the camera frame. I live a couple of blocks from that triple junction of Fairfax, Olympic, and San Vicente; I walk or drive across it every day. The house in which I live is to the right of those undeveloped boulevards, or it would be, if the image reached that far. Here, we get another glimpse of what's beneath the surface ... or beyond the lens. My building, after all, dates from 1923, as do many of the surrounding duplexes, which means the area was not as empty as it appears. Often I wonder about its history, who lived and died in these rooms where I linger with my wife and children, where I write these words. Ghosts, again, like those who haunt Mulholland's office, although these ones are more tame. Or maybe it's that they don't need to assert themselves, since they are already home.

Sidewalking

I wanted flat land I could shape.

Walt Disney

Imagine the Grove on a Wednesday morning, before business starts. Maybe it's overcast, marine inversion layer thick above the Fairfax district, morning cool, damp almost, gray as a city street. The Grove is empty but not silent; there are people here. Crack-of-dawn joggers, a woman walking her dog—in repose, the place resembles not so much a shopping center as part of a neighborhood.

Now imagine the Grove at the height of the weekend: Saturday or Sunday afternoon. It is packed (according to Caruso Affiliated Holdings, the company that owns and operates the property, eighteen million people walk through annually, more than visit Disneyland, and they spend, on average, in excess of one hundred dollars per visit), dense with shoppers and sidewalk strollers, diners chattering at outdoor restaurants. In front of the movie theater, ticket holders gather, while others drift in and out of Nordstrom's, Victoria's Secret, Barnes and Noble, the Apple Store. There are all kinds of people—black, white, Latino, Asian, young and old—and although most have come to shop,

something else is happening as well. By the large central foun-
tain, parents and kids watch the dancing waters, or sprawl across
the self-styled village green to listen to an oldies band. If you
squint a little, you almost get the impression of a quasi-public
space, commercial yes, but also communal in its way. This, of
course, is part of the point. "People come to the Grove," Rick
Caruso, the multi-millionaire developer behind the project,
once told me, "and they're spending half the day. They may not
buy a thing—most of them do, thank God—but they're coming
to hang out, run into friends, grab a cup of coffee and that, I
think, is more in line with the way people live. It feels natural."
Natural? To use a word like that in reference to the Grove seems
something of an overstatement. "The Grove's popular success,"
Alan A. Loomis wrote in 2002 on the website of the Los Angeles
Forum for Architecture and Urban Design, "reinforces entertainment retail (retail-tainment) as the only legitimate activity
for creating urban places." Still, its popularity has a lot to do
with the illusion of naturalness, the idea that what it presents is
a taste of something that resembles city life.

City life—or a version of it—is what the Grove claims to offer,
albeit in a highly mediated way. It is the kind of place I'm wired
to hate: ersatz, a contrivance, a cross between a mall and Main
Street USA at Disneyland, which is, perhaps, the most obvious
precursor to the place. (Caruso claims Walt Disney as a hero,
calling him "one of the true geniuses in the world.") And yet, I
don't hate it, not really, although I wouldn't say I love or even like
it; more accurate to label me, again, ambivalent. On the one hand,
it's impossible not to see the Grove for what it is, what Norman
Klein has called a "scripted space." With its landscaping, its
vaguely Italianate side streets and multiplex designed to resemble a classic motion picture palace, it exists at the intersection of

the town square and the movie set, a vision of a past that never was. Still, it's not necessarily nostalgia the Grove is selling … or, at least, not nostalgia alone. Sure, there's all that Disney-like manipulation, the fantasy of what Caruso calls a "real perfect little place, a place that people hope for in their own backyards"— but it is also a street (or something that looks like a street) designed for the purpose of encouraging commerce, moving merchandise, boulevard as commodity exchange. Sidewalking, in other words, a bit of slang that refers to merchants standing outside their establishments, appealing to pedestrians to come and buy. "The Grove's success," explains Diego Cardoso, a Metro official who once sat on the Los Angeles Planning Commission, "has to do with the value of creating place as an element in getting people to go and stay. It looks like a street, but it isn't public. You go to shop and to be entertained." The distinction can be encapsulated in a simple analogy: "If you look at a photograph of a city taken in 1900," Klein points out, "you'll see crowds of people, but they're all trying to get off the street because they're going somewhere. In a scripted environment, the street itself is the destination. When you make the promenade the purpose of urban life, you're missing the point of why it's there in the first place. Older cities were more nervously dynamic than that."

Los Angeles, however, is not an older city; to understand that, we only need to look at *its* photographs. In 1900, this part of town was covered with bean fields; an image shot at Fairfax and Sunset reveals rows of sweet peas stretching north towards a lone farmhouse, while Melrose Avenue was still a dirt road overhung with trees. No crowds, no streets, nowhere to go: no city, in other words, beyond downtown. This may be why L.A. remains so susceptible to constructed environments such as the Grove; its history goes back to Olvera Street and Chinatown, and encompasses such contemporary iterations as Universal CityWalk, Two Rodeo, and the Bunker Hill Steps (loosely modeled on Rome's Spanish Steps) across Fifth Street from the Central Library. Even the Farmers Market, which became a rallying point for anti-growth activists when it was announced, in the late 1990s, that the Grove (then in the process of being developed) would force relocation of its iconic clock tower, was itself a scripted landscape from a prior generation, a reconstruction of a farmer's market, built for economics and effect.

Where the Grove is different, though, is in regard to how we use it—how we reinvent it on our terms. This is what makes it interesting, essential even: that it is (inadvertently or otherwise) a laboratory, a training ground. I want to be careful of the claim I'm making because I understand that this is not its purpose, although as with any urban project, what's important are less the intentions of its builder than its integration into the life of the city of which it is a part. In that sense, the Grove reminds me of the chimerical downtown trolley project, since both offer a strategy for imagining a passage back to the future, to L.A. before it got derailed. "Most historic portions of Los Angeles were created by Pacific Electric," notes Cardoso. "Many pedestrian corridors—Santa Monica, Long Beach, Huntington Park, Glendale, Whittier, Burbank—grew out of Pacific Electric hubs." It's no coincidence, in that sense, that one of the key draws of the Grove (for visitors of a certain age) is the double-decker trolley that traverses a loose circuit through the mall. In 2013, at a Miracle Mile Chamber of Commerce meeting, Caruso floated the idea of extending the trolley in a two-mile loop, west on Third Street to the Beverly Center and south on Fairfax to the County Museum. "When you look at the other great cities," he told the chamber, "San Francisco, Portland, Seattle, just to name a few

... they all have rail streetcars. Los Angeles has so little in this regard." It's a telling statement for what it suggests about Caruso's vision for the city, as well as for what it means, or might mean, for the community.

The Grove, after all, fancies itself part of the neighborhood; it's in the nature of the design. Caruso has been explicit about that: "It's very dependent, what we do, on the neighborhood," he insists. "The neighborhood drives the design, it drives the layout, it drives the function, all of that." At the same time, his intentions are somewhat grander, as embodied by his use of that word *great*. It's a word that comes up often in his conversation, the idea of a great city, of a great street. "I love hanging out," he says, "and people-watching and feeling like you're in a mix of things going on. You go to New York and you feel like you're in the right place. That's what I was trying to tap into on these properties. I'm much more driven not by creating great retail space but by creating great civic space." Left unspoken is the question of how (or even whether) great civic space is created, if it can be invented whole cloth or if it needs to evolve. Such an issue may seem simple on the surface, but really it's a key conundrum, not just when it comes to the Grove—which, with its mix of consumer elements and communal landscape, blurs the line between mall and community—but also to Los Angeles as a whole. What does it mean when a setting such as this is constructed and controlled by a company whose goals may not be consistent with those of the community? What is the relationship between private and public space? Sidewalking again, which is, of course, a paradox, or more accurately a conflation, a funhouse mirror through which the city reflects itself.

Take the trolley as an example. In the decade since it opened, the Grove has caused huge traffic problems in its neighborhood.

The intersection of Third and Fairfax, never great to begin with, becomes impassable at peak hours. On the surface, the trolley might seem a mitigating factor, but is that really true? "There's so much traffic now," argues Diana Plotkin, president of the Beverly Wilshire Homes Association, "that the residents can't even use the major streets. I can't even imagine how much worse it would be if you run a rail line right down the middle of Third Street." As much as I love the idea of the trolley, the throwback urbanity of it, Plotkin makes an excellent point. And yet, for Caruso, it's not practicality that is the key attraction, but rather spectacle, image, the concept of how a (so-called) great city is supposed to look and work. "The premise," he explains, referring to the Grove, "has always been that we are building a great street." As for what this means: "We go around the world. We studied Michigan Avenue, the rhythm of the trees relative to the light poles, the planting areas, the width of the sidewalk. We went to Savannah, which has a great street system. We've been everywhere." The intent is to borrow elements from other places—King Street in Charleston, Newbury Street in Boston—and adapt them into what is, in essence, a virtual hybrid, the imagined facsimile of an urban landscape that might have been developed "in the 1940s, after the Farmers Market was built." This is a revealing statement, for it indicates the extent to which reality and illusion are meant to blend in this type of construction, leaving us with a tableau (there is no other word for it) whose history is both invented and, somehow, organic at once. "If we're going to build a great street," Caruso continues, "it needs to do everything a street would do, which means from a design standpoint, you have to have the right height curb and you have to have the right crown on the street and all of those things."

One of "those things," of course, is walking, the creation of a pedestrian corridor. This is implicit in the ideal of an urban environment—curbs and gutters, streetlights, a variety of storefronts—built to a distinctly human scale. "Cities have always offered anonymity, variety, and conjunction," Rebecca Solnit writes in *Wanderlust: A History of Walking*, "qualities best basked in by walking: one does not have to go into the bakery or the fortune teller's, only to know that one might." What Solnit is referring to is possibility, which is (for me, anyway) the entire reason we live in cities. The thrill of them, the electric charge of the streets . . . this has everything to do with, as Solnit puts it, the fact that cities contain "more than any inhabitant can know," that they make "the unknown and the possible spurs to the imagination." If it seems a contradiction to seek such possibility, such wonder, in a development like the Grove, this is one of the primary disruptions, the unlikely juxtapositions, that define Los Angeles. Such a seeming contradiction is at the heart of the city's ongoing reconceptualization, its slow but steady (re-)acclimatization to its streets as public space.

Let's go back to the architecture, which has been the vehicle of so many misreadings; what do we see if we peel back the surfaces a little bit? L.A. is, has always been, an architectural hotbed: Frank Lloyd Wright, Rudolf Schindler, the Case Study Houses, *Art and Architecture* magazine. Nor is this just a matter of heritage: think of Thom Mayne, Frank Gehry, Eric Owen Moss. Moss's most significant work may be the Hayden Tract, a once-derelict strip of industrial wasteland in Culver City that has become an open-air architecture showplace, with more than thirty structures erected or planned, all funded by the private developers Frederick and Laurie Samitaur Smith. Since construction began in 1986, the Hayden Tract has been regarded largely as an oddity:

a cluster of idiosyncratic buildings, known collectively as Conjunctive Points, which draw attention to themselves as works of art. (One, the Beehive, looks like, yes, an enormous beehive; another, the Stealth Building, resembles the vast wing of a military plane.) "There is a real fluidity to the urbanism of a city like L.A.," Moss told *Los Angeles Times* architecture critic Christopher Hawthorne for a profile in *Metropolis* magazine. "It would be very hard to try this in New York, Chicago, or even San Francisco. But this city is much less stratified."

And yet, as Los Angeles continues to reinvent itself, the strangeness of the Hayden Tract gets integrated into the urban core. With the opening of the Expo Line in 2012, it has become instantly more accessible; the Culver City station is a couple of blocks away. As a result, Hawthorne observes, the development "promises to set the stage for a fascinating clash of philosophies: the private, market-driven approach of the Samitaur Smiths coming face-to-face with L.A.'s newly expanding public realm." This is an essential point, since from the outset, the Hayden Tract has operated in precisely this middle ground, "designed as a sort of private urbanism. Though the buildings remade by Moss were examples of extroverted architecture, as a district, as a piece of the city, the project turned inward on itself. It remained thoroughly unknown to many Angelenos. The attitude of the Samitaur Smiths, according to Moss, has always been, 'We don't want city money, we don't want city input, we don't want city support—all we want is, leave us alone.'"

Such an attitude is quintessential to Los Angeles, evoking, as it does, the small-d democratic impulse of the place. L.A. has long sold itself as a territory of individual dreams, individual freedom, as a place where, if you have the resources, you can do what you want as you want in a home or office built to the specifications of your fantasies. Here we see what West got wrong in *The Day of the Locust*, where Capote and Mailer reveal their bourgeois, Eastern sensibilities. That we live in a city where restaurants come in the shape of derby hats or giant hot dogs, where people build themselves chateaus and fairy tale cottages or even, like the Hayden Tract and Frank Gehry's private dwellings, places that seem devoid of tradition except, perhaps, that of the imagination, is the whole idea. I don't mean to suggest Los Angeles is in any way an open city, that the tensions, the dislocations, of other urban environments do not apply. The history of the city is a history of disruptions based largely on race and class. But the flip side, the counterpoint, is that it is also a land of opportunity, even to those for whom opportunity has elsewhere been curtailed. That is why, beginning in World War II, during what has come to be known as "the Second Great Migration," the African American population of L.A. exploded, from 63,700 in 1940 to 763,000 in 1970. This was not always, or even often, a smooth transition; Chester Himes, for one, wrote that Los Angeles "hurt me racially as much as any city I have ever known— much more than any city I remember in the South." In his first novel *If He Hollers Let Him Go*, published in 1945, Himes traces that sensibility through the character of Bob Jones, a black transplant from Ohio working in a San Pedro shipyard. Bob is electric with anger, but also aware of how L.A., the space of it, allows him to assert himself, albeit in a limited way. "I had a '42 Buick Roadmaster I'd bought four months ago," he tells us, "right after I'd gotten to be a leader man, and every time I got behind the wheel and looked down over the broad, flat, mile-long hood I thought about how the rich white folks out in Beverly couldn't even buy a new car now and got a certain satisfaction." That car—another vehicle by which outsiders denigrate what they see as the city's rootless culture—becomes, on one level anyway, an expression of identity, of dignity.

It's for this reason, I'd suggest, that authenticity is such a complicated issue: not because the city's surfaces are so beguiling but because they conceal such depths. Until very recently, L.A.'s great architecture has mostly been private, or, like the Hayden Tract, in some amorphous middle ground between the private and the public, which is a territory the Grove also occupies. Think about downtown, which with the exception of City Hall and Union Station is not particularly notable for its landmarks ... or wasn't until Gehry's Walt Disney Concert Hall opened in October 2003. Setting aside the name, which is, as it has ever been, cringe-worthy, Disney Hall is a remarkably visible piece of public architecture, part of a shift that also includes the Cathedral of Our Lady of the Angels (dedicated eleven months before) and the Caltrans District 7 headquarters, built in 2004 by Mayne's Morphosis group and known, in some circles, as the Death Star for its sleek gray surfaces and skin of photovoltaic cells. Like them or hate them—and I am, I will admit, no fan of the cathedral, with its boxy yellow lack of consequence— I have little doubt that this new attention to architecture as an expression of civic identity signals changes in the cityscape at large. There are a lot of reasons, I think, why Los Angeles has had such difficulty engaging with its streets as public space, beginning with its history—the sprawl and the commuter culture, the primacy of private life. But it also has to do with the fact that for much of L.A.'s recent history, *there has been nothing to look at*, whether in the sense of institutions such as the County Museum, which spent decades turning its back to the sidewalk, or in regard to what has been a nondescript and undistinguished building stock. What is a city, after all, if not a "scripted space"—

not in the sense of manipulation, exactly, but rather in the interplay of elements (architecture, density, the serendipity of the pedestrian) that create a three-dimensional environment? This is what Caruso understands, the source of his fascination with the great street, the great city, and if his taste is more contrived, more about the managed experience than, say, Solnit's "anonymity, variety, and conjunction," this is in keeping with other, more vaguely public developments such as L.A. Live or Grand Park, a twelve-acre greensward opened in 2012 as part of the long-delayed Grand Avenue Project, paid for by the developer Related Companies and administered by the Music Center, which borders the park on its western edge.

Seen through such a filter, the Grove, which opened in 2002, becomes part of an unmediated movement, or more accurately, a series of confluences, a process not so much directed as concentric, arising out of the same set of factors, of negotiations, that have fueled other shifts. This can be easy to overlook, for Caruso operates out of a different tradition, one that begins—despite his assertion that "I didn't grow up in the real estate industry. I didn't grow up in the mall industry"—with Universal CityWalk, which became the first of what I think of as pseudo-urban mall developments when it opened in 1993. CityWalk has its antecedents, most notably the Century City Shopping Center and Marketplace (now Westfield Century City), a product of the same 1960s ideal of urban development that led the Community Redevelopment Agency to flatten and re-landscape Bunker Hill. And yet, despite its outdoor layout, its aspirations to the flow (if not the openness) of public space, Century City is another breed of shopping center altogether, one that has not aged especially well. A more appropriate precedent may be the Third Street Promenade in Santa Monica, which also has its roots in the 1960s, when three blocks of the urban core were closed to cars. Here, we see the "gentle repression" of the scripted space: a public street remade as destination, with the single goal of encouraging commerce. As the promenade has grown increasingly homogenized—in the wake of the 1994 Northridge earthquake, a number of buildings were red-tagged, clearing the way for upmarket chains such as H&M, Anthropologie, and the Gap—it offers its own variation on the unresolved relationship in Los Angeles between public and private space.

All this calls into question the extent to which—if at all— urban landscape can be created, mixed and matched as if it were a matter of fashion, or money, alone. That gets more complicated when we look at a second Caruso development, Glendale's Americana at Brand, which opened in 2008 and is like the Grove on steroids: it features 238 rental apartments and 100 condos, further eclipsing the boundary between construction and community. According to Caruso, much of Americana is patterned after Newbury Street, which he calls an almost perfect representation of how a great street is supposed to work. "What we kept studying on Newbury," he explains,

> is the ability of the retail band to carry the residential band. Old buildings did it in a very neat way. New buildings are flat, so the developer saves money. He's got his retail façade and he puts his residential façade on exactly the same plane. What we're doing in Glendale, we set that back. It's more expensive to do, but the old buildings always had a difference between where you lived and where you worked. And I thought that was a very important signal people were making at the turn of the century that a home was a home and work was work.

It's a revealing statement, not least because of the implication *(it's more expensive to do)* that some things are more important than money—not at all what you'd expect a mall operator to say. Before we get caught up in the rhetoric, however, we should note that the Americana does not look like Newbury Street, nor does it have any of the older street's organic urgency. As with many of the streets Caruso lionizes, Newbury grew up as it did for a variety of reasons, including the size and shape of Boston, the availability (or lack thereof) of transportation, and the exigencies of a different world. It has nothing to do with Glendale or Los Angeles, where mixed-use development is a relatively new innovation in a landscape traditionally zoned for single-use. This is the knock (or one of them) on places such as the Grove or the Americana, that what they offer is less a real experience than a broadly imagined facsimile, sanitized and monitored, in which not only architecture but geography, chronology, and, indeed, the very purpose of the street has been corrupted, recalibrated as an expression of our consumerist desires.

What does that mean to the city? For a hint, we need only return to the Hayden Tract. Here, too, we find ourselves in a landscape reconstructed to the specifications of its developers, less organic (let's say) than contrived. The "gentle repression" of the Hayden Tract is not necessarily economic, and yet, it is without doubt a scripted space. Conversely, the proximity of the Expo Line can't help but open up the project, making it less the property, or the function, of the entities that created it and more that of everyone. The same is true throughout Southern California, where until recently one had to drive to walk. Melrose Avenue, Venice Beach, Griffith Park, even the Third Street Promenade ... all are served by lots and parking structures, as is, of course, the Grove. "We're pulling seventy-eight zip codes to the Grove on a consistent basis," Caruso acknowledges, even as he avers that "when we build a project, the project is ours.

Then, very quickly the project isn't ours anymore—it starts getting owned by the community. All of a sudden, the surrounding influences change the character and nature of the project and you have to go with what the consumer and the neighborhood is doing with your project. Unless it's going sideways on you." What he's describing is the peculiar tension of Los Angeles, a city of both neighborhoods and sprawl. And yet, I find myself compelled by that notion of *going sideways*, which evokes the serendipity of an urban environment that shapeshifts for a million different reasons, as we interact with it in a million different ways. Just look, for instance, at Mariachi Plaza in Boyle Heights, where the opening of a Gold Line station in 2009 has helped revitalize the neighborhood, reframing it as a meeting place, a *zócalo*.

This is one of the reasons Caruso's trolley remains compelling, despite the resistance of the community. By 2023, the Metro Purple Line—which splits from the Red Line at Wilshire/Vermont and continues west to Wilshire and Western—will extend to La Cienega Boulevard, with a further expansion into Westwood scheduled to open in 2035. On the one hand, that feels like an eternity, especially to someone who once advocated for a subway station on his block. At the same time, the creation of a Wilshire/Fairfax station, across from the County Museum and within walking distance of my house, feels like a transformation so substantial that our experience of the city may be rendered fresh. With the museum as a terminus, Caruso's trolley begins to look like a western variant of the loop envisioned for downtown: a private project, yes, driven by business as opposed to civic interests, but with the potential for a similar effect. In my more sanguine moments, I imagine it as a mechanism for a coherent version of Los Angeles, in which transportation networks link to pedestrian corridors and a reconfigured urban territory evolves.

Partly, this has to do with my wishes, my desires, my vision of the city in which I want to live—the Manhattanite rising to the surface again. And yet, even Manhattan, observes Greg Hise, a professor of history at the University of Nevada, Las Vegas, who spent many years at USC's School of Policy Planning and Development, is not what we imagine it to be. "The organic city we admire so much in places like New York," Hise insists, "is itself an invention. The city we take for granted was built." Seen through such a filter, we have no choice but to look beyond our preconceptions, our judgments of what is real and what is illusion, to recognize that the city, *any* city, is created. I remember the moment I realized Manhattan was outdoors, in the sense of being underlain with dirt and stone. I was fifteen or sixteen, walking down Fifth Avenue in midtown, surrounded by those enormous temples of consumption: Rockefeller Center, St. Patrick's Cathedral, Saks Fifth Avenue. On all sides, buses, taxis, pedestrians … I could barely see my feet. Talk about a constructed environment: even the trees come dressed in concrete overshoes. At some point, I came across a building site, or a break in the pavement—I no longer recall the details—a tear in the veneer of the city through which nature (suddenly, stunningly) revealed itself. Los Angeles is full of such diversions ("scratch the surface a little and the desert shows through," Bertolt Brecht sniffed in 1941, in what may be the most vivid line ever written about the place). It's one of the reasons people come here, to walk in Runyon Canyon, to surf at Zuma, to hike the trails and feel the dislocation of a city that doesn't feel entirely like a city, even though we understand that it is. Still, what is the difference between Fifth Avenue and the La Brea Tar Pits, if both are somehow framed and bounded by our use? Only this, perhaps: that in New York, we take urbanity for granted, whereas in Los Angeles, we are still learning its vernacular.

In that sense, we may be better off considering not what the city is, its nature, so to speak, but rather what it signifies. It's less authenticity that is the issue, since there is no such thing as an organic city, than how we engage, or don't, the interactions that the place inspires. Here, we return to proportion, to the idea of building to pedestrian dimensions, which is a major factor in the success of Americana and the Grove. Place-making, in other words (Caruso likes to call himself "a place-maker"), in which the constructedness, the context, is key to the exercise. "It's the element of human scale," Cardoso says of the Grove, "absolutely, that creates the comfort level—that, and the fact that it is safe and well-controlled." The scale to which he is referring is that of the neighborhood, a scale with which we intuitively feel at home. Is this manipulative? How could it not be? All the same, Hise points out, even the most "authentic" neighborhoods (Newbury Street, refashioned as a shopping mecca; Wilshire Boulevard, with its food trucks and art installations) come to us as side-walked environments, packaged and sold. "We need to get away from this kind of binary thinking," he argues, "and think about where people feel free, where they feel part of the public. The neighborhood is an essential factor in how people think of cities, and we should look critically at what it means."

That's a radical idea, the insistence on the neighborhood, but at the same time, the least radical idea of all. It recalls the roots of this city, of any city, in the conglomeration of community, as well as the many ways in which we read the streets, the landscape, the overlapping of multiple narratives. The temptation is to write off Caruso's rhetoric as the stuff of platitude, but if his sensibility remains business-driven, there is something more at work. The Grove, after all, is a neighborhood *in his imagination*—"a place," as he puts it, "that people hope for in their own backyards." If this seems more than a little hyperbolic (an echo, perhaps, of his hero Disney), it also suggests its own unlikely authenticity. By invoking the backyard, Caruso touches on a cornerstone of Southern California living: the single-family home, the private aesthetic, Adamic's "enormous village" again. And yet, that vision belongs to the old Los Angeles, the one that spreads out and not up, the city of sprawl and not community, the one that doesn't any longer work. More important is where we go from here, how we move back to more traditional urban models, and come to think in terms of public, as opposed to private, life. That the Grove is not intended to provoke such questions does not mean it doesn't provoke them anyway, simply by the way it asks (requires?) us to interact. "The importance of public space," Cardoso says, "is as a place we go without knowing each other to enhance our relationships as citizens and public beings." This is where Caruso's point of view begins to merge with Hise's, both reimagining the city from the sidewalk up. That this is essential should go without saying; even in the Wilshire corridor—which is among the city's densest residential districts—many streets are defined by setback shopping centers, such as the one on the southeast corner of Third and Fairfax, directly across from the Grove, and they remain a source of Los Angeles' great alienation, streets that don't engage with the sidewalk, that suffer from an inequity of scale. "The sidewalk," Cardoso says, "is very important to creating common ground."

This is what the Grove aspires to do, although it comes with paradoxes of its own. Most fundamental is that, in seeking to replicate the dynamic of a neighborhood, it separates itself from the neighborhood, and not only in regard to all that traffic, all those zip codes, all that congestion, which the trolley (if it ever gets constructed) may exacerbate. Unlike Americana, the Grove does not engage the surrounding streets, offering only large walls papered with advertisements—hardly an enticement to draw foot traffic from outside. This, Caruso says, was at least partly merchant driven. "One thing that really fascinated me," he recalls, "was that when we first designed the project, we had some storefronts out on Third Street. And every one of the retailers said, 'No, no, no—we want our storefront on the inside.'" Equally significant, the Grove remains, despite all the talk of civic space, a private development, with a clearly stated code of conduct and consequences for those who can't abide. "You're not going to have activities here that you have on Third Street Promenade," Caruso declares. "You're not going to have twelve people juggling sticks of salami. You're not going to have crime, you're not going to have graffiti. There are limits on the activities and your ability to do whatever you want to do on the property." And yet, if that frames the Grove as something of an experiment in social engineering, this, too, has been part of L.A.'s history all along. Beverly Hills, Westwood, Leimart Park, and even, or especially, Miracle Mile—all were initially conceived as real estate, products of commercial will. "The public street," Hise reminds us, "was not fundamentally a place of liberation. Where was this golden moment? Most history tells us it never existed, that there were always people who couldn't participate." Again, I am reminded of the 2006 immigration rallies, which, whatever else they achieved, functioned as an act of reclamation, an expression as essential to what is happening in Los Angeles as the construction of the Red Line or the opening of Disney Hall. "Regardless of how these spaces are designated," Hise explains, referring to all of it, from the Grove to the subway to downtown, "their identity has to do with how they're taken over by the public. And that's indicative of people's aspirations and desires."

Considered on such terms, what may be most compelling about the Grove is that we must learn to read it, how to use it, that none of us—perhaps Caruso most of all—has any real idea of what it means. It is a scripted space, absolutely, a temple of consumerism, yet it is also a conflation, a contradiction, an elaborate hybrid. Does it seem as if I'm making too much of this? Maybe so. But like so much in L.A., the Grove challenges me to set aside my preconceptions, my ideology and aesthetics, and examine through a broader lens. Take my children as an example: growing up in the neighborhood, they had their first urban experiences, such as they were, wandering Caruso's "great street," with its trolley, its gentle arch of pavement and its measured setbacks, its building façades like those of a theme park, a theme park that turns out to be real. For my wife and me, it represented a safe zone, halfway between home and public boulevard, a place we could leave them for a few hours, at ten and eleven, where they might puzzle out some of the terrors and the pleasures of city life. As a child, I found these sorts of interactions transformative, to my understanding both of place and of myself. Indeed, one of the finest aspects of growing up in Manhattan was the opportunity it afforded to walk the streets, anonymous and somehow equal, no longer quite a kid if not yet an adult. Such opportunities seemed unavailable (or difficult to come by) in Los Angeles the first decade we were here. Then the Grove opened, and beneath its contrivances, its willful constructedness, I began to imagine that something real could happen ... if nothing else, a whisper of street level interaction, no matter how controlled. "Urbanism," Rebecca Solnit once suggested, "is a learned behavior, not an infrastructure design. And a development like the Grove might offer an education in the uses and pleasure of outdoor space, which people have to have."

Education in the uses and pleasure of outdoor space: yes, I want to say, that's it precisely, what the Grove offers, in spite of itself. It is a manufactured cityscape that becomes authentic by virtue of how it is used. It is a private landscape, a commercial development, that also functions as quasi-public space. To engage with it, we must recalibrate our thinking, in much the same way that, to engage with Los Angeles, we must recalibrate our thinking—about cities and how they work as well as about the nature of public/private partnerships, which are and will be (for better and for worse) increasingly a factor in the way urban environments operate. In 2009, the California State Senate passed a law allowing Caltrans, Metro, and other transit agencies to enter public/private partnerships for infrastructure projects; these include the downtown trolley, for which, as the *Los Angeles Times* reported in September 2014, the city had begun seeking private partners to make up a one hundred million dollar funding gap. For Caruso, partnership is not the issue—he is operating on his own. But that, too, suggests the symbiotic relationship between public and private space. "The most fascinating thing to me about real estate," he says, "is that it's not about real estate, it's about public policy. The good developers understand how public policy drives private development and how private development has to work within the realms of public policy and push the envelope a little bit here and there." What that means in terms of public space, perhaps, is that if you build it, they will come. "What public space do we have in Los Angeles?" Caruso asks. "Century City? Designed for the automobile, not for the person. You have to make the city more livable for the pedestrian. Isn't it ironic that private space is opened to the public and not the other way around? It's ass backwards in this town."

That is the essential question, the puzzle at the heart of how Los Angeles sees itself. From 2012 to 2014, the city built twenty-four vest-pocket parks in vacant lots and other corners, but even so, reports the Trust for Public Land, only 52.5 percent of Angelenos live within ten minutes walking distance of such public space. Indeed, L.A. ranks thirty-third among American cities in walkable access to its parkland—a clear sign that pedestrianism is not yet here to stay. In that regard, what the Grove provides may be a testing ground, inadvertent though it may be: a place where the community, the neighborhood, can learn, or relearn, sidewalking, street life. It's a conundrum, that in an ersatz space real things happen, and yet, isn't that part of the point? "It's why we don't have gates," Caruso says. "If we're going to build a great street, it needs to do everything a street would do, which means you don't have gates. You keep it open. The more we do that, the more you become part of the fabric of the city." There is, of course, a lot that's weird or troublesome about that statement. It overlooks the very real issues of what happens in a private space designed to appear public, not to mention what is disallowed. There will never be a protest march at the Grove, nor any political activism, nor any expression of dissent at all. The diversity it attracts—and among its millions of shoppers are dozens of ethnicities and demographics: Latino, Asian, African American, Anglo, upper, middle, lower income—is determined by the mercantile nature of the experience; no one is there who doesn't have money to spend. And yet, and yet, and yet ... what we learn, or relearn, here, the serendipitous encounter, the random meeting, the flow of the crowd, the friend you haven't seen in years, is a part of the way cities work, the way cities are supposed to work. Let's not call it urban space; let's call it urban *psychic* space, a more amorphous idea, harder to pin down. We are, in other words, creating the psyche of the city, which means that what resonates is less the intent of a space such as the Grove than the ways we occupy it, and in so doing, render it our own.

Imagine the Grove, then, in two decades, maybe three, when its run as L.A.'s uber-mall has ended, and it has settled into the long second act of urban life. Perhaps it will be run down, need a facelift, a reinvention, like the Beverly Center a mile to the west. Perhaps the neighborhood will have changed and the Grove with it, much as during the last eighty years, the Farmers Market has been continually transformed. Regardless, here's what we can count on: the lives of cities are open-ended, a matter of framing and reframing that is tough to anticipate. Caruso, it is said, got the idea for the Grove from Rome's Via Veneto, where he saw centuries-old buildings redeveloped for commercial use. That's a striking image, suggesting not just that his intentions may be more complex than he's given credit for, but also that our cities supersede us, that they are independent entities in which we only play a part.

Mapping History

Every city has a metaphorical geography that
determines and reflects the nature of its growth.

William Fox

One quiet evening late in summer, I leave the house and wander
five blocks north, crossing against the light *(Oh, I see, we're playing
by New York rules today)* at San Vicente, cutting through the
streets north of the Olympia Medical Center, a cluster of blocks,
made up almost entirely of single family houses from the 1920s
and 1930s, that remains the embodiment of the horizontal downtown. Ahead, the scattered towers of Mid-Wilshire: the vertical
black rectangle of City National Bank, the rigid glass and concrete stripes of 5900 Wilshire, once the Variety building but
now renamed for the hotel and entertainment company SBE,
and at thirty-two stories the tallest structure by a long shot on
this stretch. Night is coming on, but it's still light enough to see
not only my footsteps on the uneven pavement, but also the
parameters of the neighborhood. I used to think about this part
of town as *generic city of L.A.*, not with any dig intended but as
a compliment, a reference to Waldie's sacred ordinariness,
Banham's plains of id. In *Los Angeles: The Architecture of Four*

Ecologies, he explains it this way: "These are the plains that are seen in the classic view south from the Griffith Park Observatory, and this view does indeed show an endless flat city—the interminable parallels of Vermont, Normandie, and Western Avenues stretching south as far as the eye can penetrate the urban haze, intersecting at absolutely precise right angles the east-west parallels of Hollywood, Sunset, and Santa Monica Boulevards. Melrose Avenue, Beverly Boulevard, Third Street, Wilshire Boulevard, under the San Mo freeway, past Exposition Park, and the campus of the University of Southern California" ... to read that litany is like walking a three-dimensional map in my own mind. "I was amazed," Christopher Isherwood wrote in 1939, on his second day in Los Angeles, "at the size of the city, and at its lack of shape. There seemed no reason why it should ever stop. Miles and miles of little houses, wooden or stucco, under a Technicolor sky." Yes, yes, but my stroll tonight reveals a bit more nuance, a sense (let's say) of neighborhood. On the sidewalks, faded chalk unveils its pastel colors: hopscotch, sunshine drawings, stick figures of boys and girls. Through the windows, I can see families eating dinner together, or cleaning up after dinner, or sitting in silence, with each other or alone. Like any place, Los Angeles is like any place: the anti-exceptionalist argument I have with myself each time I walk these streets. Once again, I am confronted by the tension between public and private, or maybe it's just me on the outside, looking in.

That tension feels slightly more acute this evening because I'm on my way to one of these houses to look at a map. Not a city map, framed and platted, but map as art, map as act of interpretation, a private expression of public concerns. I met the owner while she was standing on this very sidewalk. I was walking home from the County Museum, another of my endless cycles,

Hauser north to Wilshire, then a slow meander through the
campus of Hancock Park: Page Museum, La Brea Tar Pits, the
site of Excavation 101, all those memories, the interplay of past
and present on the cityscape. This is as close as I come to deep
history in Los Angeles, deep personal history; I took my children through here countless Saturdays and Sundays when they
were younger, watching the archeologists, murmuring over
bones and tar. I recall the dioramas of the Page Museum,
although I haven't been inside in better than a decade, skeletons
that grow fur and muscle definition as you shift the angle of your
viewing, then fade back into skeletons again. It's impossible—or
impossible for *me*—not to read them as a metaphor for the temporary nature of our duration, the slow stripping away, the erasure that will obliterate every one of us. And yet, that is their
charm and resonance. The Tar Pits are one of the few things I
remember about L.A. from my childhood, along with the oil
wells that dotted (still dot) the Baldwin Hills stretch of La
Cienega like prehistoric birds. There is a photograph, taken in
1967 or 1968, of me at six, standing before the plaster mammoths
on the shoreline, staring at them as if they were real. This was
during the year my father had a fellowship in Downey and we
lived in Long Beach: source, perhaps, of my California fascination all along. What lingers for me is the wonder of it, the sense
(although I wouldn't then have had the language to describe it) of
time collapsing, all those ages, all those eons, overlapping,
becoming in some weird way one.

Here, we have a rebuttal to the trope that Los Angeles has no
history: how can we say that when, for more than twenty years
after I moved here, there were two plastic sawhorses, embla-
zoned with *Department of Public Works, Street Services*, at the south-
west corner of Curson and Wilshire, to steer pedestrians clear of

the tar that bubbles at the curb? There is one set of human remains at the Page Museum: La Brea Woman, the skeleton of a woman who died nine thousand years ago, head stoved in with a blunt object, a hole in the top of her skull. "Paleontologists," explains Amy Wilentz in *I Feel Earthquakes More Often Than They Happen*, "believe that she died a violent death outside the tar pits and was then tossed in"—a circumstance that feels at once surprisingly contemporary and unsurprisingly human. And yet, lest this seem to suggest some sort of historical continuity, Wilentz cautions otherwise. "Although the skull attached to the skeleton is a cast of La Brea Woman's actual skull," she tells us, "the rest of the skeleton belonged to a modern Pakistani female, according to museum officials, and was purchased by L.A.'s Natural History Museum from Ward's Natural Science back when Ward's still sold actual human remains. The Pakistani woman's skeleton was then colored to resemble the dark bronze coloring of bones that have aged in tar, and the femurs were shortened and put back together to achieve an approximation of La Brea Woman's small stature.... So from start to finish, the person I knew as La Brea Woman was a phony, a creation of fabulists and liars."

The same, of course, might be said about the Tar Pits, which, in the grand Los Angeles tradition of Olvera Street, of Chinatown and the Farmers Market, are an invention of their own. Originally part of the Mexican land grant of Rancho La Brea, the acreage was deeded to Henry Hancock in 1860 (hence, the name of the park as well as the statue of Hancock's son George, who donated the land to the county in 1924); the main site was an asphalt mine until it and other pits were excavated between 1910 and 1915. One more thing to love about Los Angeles, and for the same reason I love so many of its other landmarks: that they are rife with contradiction, conflating artificiality and authenticity.

1915 was a century ago, which may as well be eternity in Southern California—when these pits were first dug out, there was
nothing here. At the same time, the history they offer is, if not
false, then a construction, like all the stories we like to tell ourselves. What is the appeal of the Tar Pits? For me, it begins with
that glimmer of childhood memory, forty-seven, forty-eight
years ago, a series of lifetimes, or so it seems. Were this another
city, New York for instance, I would have dozens if not hundreds
of these images, but in L.A., there is (for me, anyway) just the
one. And yet, how often do I think about that memory in the
course of my peregrinations? Four times a week, five times a
week, I walk this campus, meandering past those static mammoths. And if I sometimes smile at what Wilentz calls their
"mangy and low-rent" cheesiness, I almost never consider what
they have to tell me—not about Los Angeles per se, but the
landscape of *my* history, my connection to this place.

This, in some sense, is the motivation behind tonight's excur-
sion: to put the collective in personal terms. The owner of the
map, a researcher at UCLA, has invited me to see it, although it's
taken a long time, a year or more, to take the short walk from my
house to hers. Our link seems loose, amorphous, if rooted also in
these streets and sidewalks: the night we met, she was talking
with a neighbor on the corner; as I passed, her companion recog-
nized me (we had been introduced, a few weeks prior, in the
museum plaza) and said hello. It was the simplest of interactions,
the kind we take for granted in most cities, although in L.A.,
such a possibility is often overlooked. One afternoon, my wife
and I shared a similar moment on Pico Boulevard near Robert-
son; we were walking when I noticed a young man following half
a dozen or so feet behind us, pace lockstepped with ours. He
didn't come off as threatening, but he did seem interested in our

conversation, which involved a trip we were planning to Chicago, in part to visit my father-in-law's grave. As we discussed options for getting to the cemetery—rent a car? take a taxi?—we heard a voice suggest the El. It was the young man, who told us he had recently moved to California from Chicago; he *had* been eavesdropping, but only, he insisted by way of reassurance, because our conversation reminded him of home. Randomness, serendipity, like meeting this woman on the sidewalk: a chain of associations that are (or should be) at the heart of city life.

That's the message of the map, I think, which hangs in a corner of the woman's living room, by turns representational and abstract. It's hand-drawn in black and colored markers on white paper; you can see the creases where the artist, Eric Brightwell—who has produced 150 maps since he started walking the city in 2008, as well as 101 related blog posts for the website of Amoeba Records—folded it to fit into his pocket as he walked. I trace the streets of the community: Sixth, Wilshire, Eighth, Olympic. I smile at the representation, in the upper left-hand corner, of the signs that mark the boundaries of the neighborhood (*Miracle Mile*, they read, in bold electric letters), one on Wilshire west of Fairfax, another west of La Brea, facing east. These are among the first elements Brightwell looks for, he will tell me later, the mani festations of a city framed in three-dimensional space. "I try to figure out if there are set borders or not," he explains of his process, although in a city as amorphous as this one—in any city, really—that's a quixotic effort, for who can say with any definition where a neighborhood begins or ends?

Miracle Mile is a case in point, since, in the most specific terms, the name applies to the mile-long stretch of Wilshire between Fairfax and La Brea, miraculous because A. W. Ross labeled it as such ninety years ago. I prefer the term Mid-Wilshire or Mid-City (which sits a mile or so to the east but bleeds over, especially when you get to Pico), or even Mid-Town, which has begun to pop up along San Vicente over the last few years. On the one hand, I'm reminded of the initiative, in the wake of the Rodney King riots, to rename some of the city's most notorious neighborhoods, in an effort to scrub them of their history. In 2003, the City Council voted to retire the designation South-Central Los Angeles, replacing it with South Los Angeles, as if such a distinction would, in the words of then-Councilwoman Jan Perry, "go a long way toward changing attitudes and how people view this community." That this is sophistry barely requires stating, and yet it remains a strategy by which way L.A. (re)defines itself. "For several years now," reported *The New York Times*, "many neighborhoods in Los Angeles and nearby cities have changed their names to distance themselves from areas with bad reputations. Sepulveda, a neighborhood in the San Fernando Valley, recently became Panorama City and North Hills. In Compton, a Los Angeles suburb infested with crime and gangs, the Crystal Park Hotel and Casino has marketed itself as being in Crystal City to attract tour groups." Not only that, but certain communities in South-Central (Green Meadows, Chesterfield Square, Morningside Heights) have taken this, or been taken by it, even further, creating what are in essence a series of micro-neighborhoods. The obvious question posed here has to do with authenticity: How can we know what a neighborhood is when we can't say for sure what it is called? That, however, overlooks the bigger point, which is about engagement: what we call a neighborhood, in other words, matters less than how it feels to live there.

In that regard, the map at which I'm gazing offers a highly particularized vision of Miracle Mile. This is both inevitable and heartening because it suggests the extent to which place and identity overlap. To the woman who owns it, the map, commissioned by her husband, is both source and illustration of connection, neighborhood refracted through a single lens. For every collective landmark (the May Company, 5900 Wilshire, the Petersen Automotive Museum, the El Rey Theatre), there are other, more specific icons: Leonardo's Nightclub on La Brea; Yuko Kitchen on South Dunsmuir; Harvey's Guss Meat Company on San Vicente; Wilshire Court, an office park edged with a small seam of green space, one more private/public compromise. The interplay is fascinating, not only between the personal and the communal but also between competing versions of the individual; when I mention that I live south of San Vicente, she tells me that's a different neighborhood. She's not wrong— my little corner of the city is known as Wilshire Vista, not to be confused with Wilshire Vista Heights and Wilshire Highlands and Little Ethiopia, all of them demarcated on Brightwell's map as a kind of negative space, *terra incognita*, the end of the known world, *here be dragons*, beware. "It's almost a map of exclusion," Brightwell explains, "defining the neighborhood by what it isn't" … although in the next breath, he is insisting that his intent is not to be programmatic but rather fluid, not unlike L.A. itself. "I'm interested in boundaries," he goes on, "but I don't want anyone to think they're walls. So sometimes I make the maps less border-specific and put in things outside the lines. When I did South-Central, I included the Coca-Cola bottling plant on Central near Pico, even though it's six blocks north of where the neighborhood ends. Anyway, who's to say what makes the neighborhood? They're calling it the Central Avenue Corridor now."

This fluidity emerges most directly in some of Brightwell's drafts of this map, which are on display across the room from the completed version. These are sketches, rough takes, less

about landmarks than framing the terrain. Neighborhoods overlap in quick, impressionistic juxtapositions: Brookside, Long-
wood Highlands, West Pico. In one, a loose bracket fills the right
side; it is labeled Mid-Wilshire. To compare this with the final
product is like holding two versions of Los Angeles in your head
at the same time, one the messy city of the imagination and the
other the more ordered grid of the streets. Each has something
to tell us about L.A., how it asserts itself. I'm particularly struck
by the white space, not only in the drafts (where it's to be
expected) but also in the finished work. For all the articulated
imagery—Hancock Park, for instance, with its looping trails
and excavations—the further south and east one looks, the emp-
tier things become. In part, that has to do with the experience of
the owner, whose interactions in the neighborhood cluster along
Wilshire; the map, after all, is designed to reflect what Miracle
Mile means to her. Yet even more, the white space speaks for all
of us, illuminating our glancing knowledge of the city, even (or
especially) the areas we occupy. "One reason," Brightwell says,
"that I leave the maps vague beyond the neighborhoods is that I
want them to be neighborhood specific. What happens outside
remains outside. But there's also a throwback to old maps,
Renaissance maps, that were highly detailed in the center and
then got increasingly vague as they radiated out. People often
have a bunker mentality, and so the maps become a way to tease
them for not knowing enough about their neighborhoods, or
what lies beyond. Los Angeles is really big, it's true, but people
often act like exploring it is too hard."

Bunker mentality recalls the mindset I first brought to Southern
California, even before I moved out of New York. Back then, as
a visitor, I'd stay with a friend in West Hollywood; every morning, we'd have coffee in his breakfast room. On the wall above

the table, he had a poster called *Los Angeles: From Space*, featuring
a satellite photo, shot in daylight, of the built environment from
a hundred miles up. These days, we take such images for
granted; the very first thing I did when I got an iPad was to
zoom in on my house with Google Earth. Cheap thrills … or
perhaps it was more connective, a way of using the big picture to
locate the smaller picture framed inside. In any case, that satellite picture is the opposite of what I'm now after, or what Brightwell is. From such distance, what emerges is a portrait of sprawl
rather than of neighborhoods, a certain point-of-view. To see
L.A. at such a distance, carpet of gray grid extending from the
ocean to the mountains, small tendrils creeping though the
passes to nourish ancillary offshoots in the San Gabriel Valley
and the Inland Empire, is to play into the archetype of chaos,
the formless growth by which development fills every corner
like a kind of moss. It used to make me think of Trantor, the
imperial capital in Isaac Asimov's *Foundation Trilogy*, a planet on
which "all the land surface …, 75,000,000 square miles in extent,
was a single city." Trantor, however, represents the essence of a
structured environment, whereas *Los Angeles: From Space* offers a
landscape that appears without shape. What's the point? For one
thing, that maps, even photographic ones, are never neutral, a
subjectivity that Brightwell embodies in his work. But even
more, it's that L.A. begins to elude us the moment we start making statements about what it means. "Though the infinite patch-
work of subdivisions and development tracts are best seen from
above," writes USC architecture professor Victor J. Jones in *(IN)
formal L.A.: The Space of Politics*, "their patterns belie the subtle
ambiguities revealed at close range. Within the endless sprawl
and spontaneous urbanism reside flurries of uncodified spatial
configurations. No high-definition map or satellite image can

accurately trace the mega-city's off-the-record events and ad hoc social formation."

The key phrase here, of course, is *ad hoc*, which—as at the Grove—has less to do with how the city is developed than how it is used. At the center of Jones's book is an essay on Watts, the South Los Angeles community that exploded during the 1965 riots, although (unlike South-Central) it was never renamed. Watts remains known for two things: those riots and the Watts Towers, an elaborate installation "handcrafted from bent rebar and caked on cement mortar carefully encrusted with little pieces of broken glass, ceramic time, and seashells in ornate mosaic patterns." The project was created by Simon Rodia, an Italian American laborer who abandoned it in 1954 after thirty-three years of work. As to why, Rodia apparently grew tired of the tensions in the neighborhood, of vandalism and suspicion on every side. One particularly ludicrous example: during World War II, the Towers, which rise nearly a hundred feet over what was once the artist's backyard, were rumored to be transmitters, used to share secrets with the Japanese. Rodia deeded the property to a neighbor and moved north to the Bay Area, to Martinez, seat of Contra Costa County; he did not look back. And yet, is it too much to suggest that in turning from L.A., Rodia became one of its exemplary citizens, because he left the most significant piece of himself behind? *Nuestro Pueblo*, he called the Towers, "our town," like Thornton Wilder in three dimensions, a monument to birth and death, to generations, to the inner life of the city, digging deeper than the surface of its streets. "I had in mind to do something big and I did it," Rodia said about his efforts, and this tells us something about not just his ambition but also his commitment, his sense of Los Angeles as a city of neighborhoods.

There's something tenacious about this effort: a self-taught artist erecting a structure no one wanted in an area people go out of their way not to find. "Not surprisingly," Jones points out, "many Angelenos never venture to this 2.5-square-mile section of southeast Los Angeles. For most, Watts resides in the collective psyche as euphemism, a one-word cautionary tale of persistent cultural, social, and economic tension." After Rodia left, the Towers became a further source of controversy, regarded by the city as "an unauthorized public hazard," unplanned, unbuilt to code. A demolition order was revoked in 1959, after they passed a lateral stress test; the Towers opened to the public the following year. "A kid could come along in his bare feet and step on this glass—not that you'd ever know," Thomas Pynchon wrote in his 1966 essay "A Journey Into the Mind of Watts":

> These kids are so tough you can pull slivers of it out of them and never get a whimper. It's part of their landscape, both the real and the emotional one: busted glass, busted crockery, nails, tin cans, all kinds of scrap and waste. Traditionally Watts. An Italian immigrant named Simon Rodia spent 30 years gathering some of it up and converting a little piece of the neighborhood along 107th Street into the famous Watts Towers, perhaps his own dream of how things should have been: a fantasy of fountains, boats, tall openwork spires, encrusted with a dazzling mosaic of Watts debris. Next to the Towers, along the old Pacific Electric tracks, kids are busy every day busting more bottles on the steel rails. But Simon Rodia is dead and now the junk just accumulates.

Nearly half a century later, Rodia's monument remains emblematic of the community, with its legacy of making something out of nothing, creating art, identity, from the detritus of daily life.

Watts, of course, is very different from Miracle Mile (or, for that matter, from most other sections of Los Angeles); according to the 2010 U.S. Census, Jones writes, "half of all families in Watts live in poverty, with an average per capita income of $6,681." What both neighborhoods share, however, is an engagement in how identity evolves. This goes deeper than renaming. Indeed, Watts has had the same name since the early twentieth century, when, as Arna Bontemps wrote in *God Sends Sunday*, "the streets ... were three or four dusty wagon paths. In the moist grass along the edges cows were staked. Broken carts and useless wagons littered the front yards of the people, carts with turkeys and game chickens and guinea fowl roosting on the spokes of the wheels and wagons from the beds of which small dark mules were eating straw." More essentially, it suggests a strategy for considering the relationship between built and social landscapes, in which the way our neighborhoods look and are arranged tells us more than a little bit about what they are. Often, we frame these issues in terms of negatives, as in the phenomenon of gated community residents voting in blocs to benefit their interests rather than those of the community—"by, for example," Carol A. Bell and Robert E. Lang have written, "gaining seats on school boards in districts where none of their children attend school, in an effort to derail new spending and thus lower their own taxes." The Watts Towers—as well as Brightwell's maps, the Tar Pits, and La Brea Woman—insist on something else. They give us what I continue to imagine as the do-it-yourself city, in which the only narratives worth considering are the ones we create ourselves.

A decade or so ago, I spent some time with the Dutch photographer Robbert Flick, who moved to Southern California in 1967. Since the early 1980s, Flick has been shooting what amounts to a series of "cognitive maps" that track different corners of the region, experimenting with juxtaposition and sequence, not to mention the constant interplay between proximity and distance, between narrow and wide points of view. For the last fifteen years, these "maps" have taken the form of large grids composed of hundreds of discreet images, which together trace the arcs of boulevards, freeways, and other cityscapes. He has worked with film, video, and now digital imagery, shooting the length of whatever thoroughfare he's traveling, generating an uninter-rupted set of pictures of the trip. Later, he'll cull individual shots that interest him or suggest something about the nature of the scene. The advantage of this apparently undigested style of image-making is that it is "continuous and, to an extent, ran-dom," which in purely practical terms, means that he has many images with which to work. Equally important are the project's theoretical underpinnings, which have everything to do with Los Angeles—its space, its freedom—as well as with the inevi-table role of chance in a mediated environment. How, after all, do we make sense of Flick's montages? How do they add up to something coherent and complete? The answer begins and ends with our experience, which, like Flick's, is constant and unend-ing, shaped by what we notice as we move throughout the city, until it becomes its own three-dimensional collage. "My experi-ence is what I agree to attend to," William James wrote in 1890. "Only those items which I notice shape my mind." L.A., then, takes shape in our efforts to observe it, to organize its jagged jumpcuts into a vision we can *recognize.*

Flick's triptych of Pico Boulevard, shot between 1994 and 1999, presents an example of this dynamic, a trio of image fields that together map the length of Pico, from Shutters on the Beach in Santa Monica, through West L.A., Beverly Hills, Pico-Robertson, Koreatown, and Pico-Union. The pieces are large—four by seven feet—and each contains several rows of individual pictures that we can follow, left to right, in much the same way as we read a text. Looking at them, one immediately understands the artist's use of the word "grid," for that's what they are, vast photographic grids, resembling the schema of the city itself. From a distance, actually, they suggest nothing so much as street plans, each rectangular image echoing a single block surrounded by narrow arteries of white space. Like the city, too, Flick's collages slip back and forth between concreteness and abstraction depending on how close or far away you stand. Move in tight and you notice the particulars: a row of storefronts yielding to an empty lot yielding to an intersection—the block-by-block sequence of the boulevard as it unspools. Here, Flick constructs what is in essence a visual narrative, giving weight to certain details by extending them across several frames. The overpass of the 10 is stretched to highlight the interplay of light and shadow, while further east, a nondescript office building receives a similar treatment, forcing us to notice what we might otherwise overlook. The idea, he explains, is "to see familiar streets decontextualized and recontextualized." Throughout the piece, he lingers on certain landmarks while downplaying others, using these juxtapositions to hint at ironies and relationships—such as the one we cannot help but posit between a club called "The Sober Inn" and a nearby liquor store.

That this mirrors the experience of walking or driving in Los Angeles is the point of the endeavor; it reflects back to us both what we notice and what we don't. Like Brightwell's maps, they reveal our eyes, our presence, as the contextualizing factors. Both projects play off the tension between the small and big picture, between the street and the more expansive assembly of which it is a part. Take a few steps back or look to the edges and suddenly you're in the presence of another landscape, where details telescope in a wash of shape and color, as if we're seeing not street scenes but broad brushstrokes of brown and blue and white. From this perspective, there is no specificity, just a succession of color fields, impressions, simultaneously blurry and sharp. Our eyes go to the line of sky, the line of traffic, all these parallel rows that add up to a city we can never recognize in full. It's as if, in framing his images, Flick is commenting on the impossibility of Los Angeles as a coherent structure—even as he offers up a different kind of coherence, albeit one that we must step away to see. This is the paradox of Los Angeles: here, order is a function of disorder, and clarity and chaos go hand in hand. Like Pico Boulevard, Flick's photographs represent a project too vast to be encompassed, one that asserts itself in pieces, if at all.

Lately, Flick has readapted his aesthetic to the changing city, shooting and reshooting his commute from USC, where he has taught for nearly forty years, to Claremont, where he lives. These collages (so to speak) recreate greater Los Angeles out of its "retinal increments": first the city streets as seen through a bus window, then the suburbs—Monterey Park to Rosemead to El Monte to West Covina to Montclair—through which the photographer passes by Metrolink train. Such a vision is both as personal as it gets (as Flick's experience of living in, of moving through, the landscape) and also inherently collective, something to which we all relate. It defines the city by reveling in its diffusion, highlighting, by turns, the neighborhoods and the sprawl. What does this mean? The answer is in the eye of the beholder, as we confront the mashup-like nature of Southern California, where we continually interpose our sensibilities on what can often seem like random fragments, *generic city of L.A.* And yet what is generic city of L.A.? It's more complicated than the phrase suggests, or so Flick means to tell us. Like Brightwell, he exposes whole territories of meaning by allowing—no, requiring—us to individualize what is in the pictures, to search out our streets, our landmarks, to interact with them on specific terms. The idea, both of them insist, is to "empathetically respond to whatever is there," which is another way of saying: keep your eyes open, look for the points of intersection where the city becomes individualized, unique.

As it happens, Flick and Brightwell share their own unlikely point of intersection: the Coca-Cola bottling plant downtown. For Brightwell, it's an emblem of how we extend, or redefine, South-Central; for Flick, a fitting endpoint to his Pico Boulevard triptych. It's a building I also adore, although I'm rarely in its presence, and yet it feels fitting that it should emerge in both artists' work as a lens. After all, in its Streamline Moderne styling—finished in 1939, it has rounded corners, portholes, and a catwalk, like some crazy landlocked ocean liner—it reminds me of nothing so much as The Darkroom, that programmatic Wilshire Boulevard camera store turned restaurant. Built one year apart, at a distance of eight miles, the two buildings seem to speak to one another, suggesting resonances we might not ordinarily recognize. If nothing else, they reanimate the notion of the do-it-yourself city, in which meaning accrues not just from the landmarks but also from how we interact with them, the way we do, or do not, connect the dots.

On that long-ago afternoon, after Flick and I had finished talking, I left the County Museum, where he had been sorting images for a retrospective, and crossed the Boulevard to 5900 Wilshire, where I was to meet a friend. I took the elevator to the twenty-fourth floor, gravitated to my friend's office window, waited as he finished a call. From this perspective, the city looked defined, orderly, laid out in neat little squares, vegetation lush and decadently green. I could almost imagine it as the expression of a larger sensibility, the end result of some collective bit of urban planning—although more than anything, it brought me back to the aesthetic of Flick's grids. It wasn't so much the regularity of the city, the way all those blocks and boulevards appeared to fit so nicely, but rather the sense of distance, of the specifics blurring, that put this in my head. That was my neighborhood down there, but from twenty-four stories up, everything faded into a wash of line and color, as if I had just stepped back from one of Flick's photographic works. For a moment, I let my eyes slip out of focus, saw the landscape blur in white and green. Then, my friend hung up the phone and broke my reverie, and I moved backwards from the window, narrowing my frame of reference once again.

For the remainder of the afternoon, I thought about the view from that window, the way it both suggested some kind of order and insisted this was largely out of reach. The city, after all, may reveal itself at a distance, but as Flick and Brightwell's work reminds us, we interact with L.A. through its streets. The larger vision is composed of smaller moments, and if we are to apprehend or to reclaim it, we must engage block by block, boulevard by boulevard. "The cumulative effect," Flick says, "will be to have all these narratives contained, like an encyclopedia. All these fragments will turn into a metaphor. And at that point, when they become a metaphor, it will answer the question of what Los Angeles is."

Miracle Mile

Even friends who had the means to help me laughed
and wished me luck.

A. W. Ross

There's a lot of hype tonight at the United Artists Theatre,
which is perhaps as it should be. Finished in 1927, as part of what
was then the United Artists building—at the time the tallest in
Southern California—it sits on Broadway just south of Ninth
Street, in a section of Los Angeles that was for many years
neglected, although it is now being rebranded as emblematic of
the ongoing revival of downtown. Half a block north is the glori-
ous Eastern building, finest structure in the city, with its tur-
quoise terra cotta façade and geometric art deco motifs. I always
think of Edmund Wilson when I see it: "the blue Avocado Building," he sniffed in *The New Republic* in 1931, a year after the Eastern
opened, "bawdy as the peacock's tail." Both structures occupy a
special place in city council member Jose Huizar's trademarked
"Bringing Back Broadway" campaign, a "Streetscape Master
Plan" developed in 2009 and implemented four years later, that,
the flackage assures us, "boldly prioritizes people over vehicles,
reducing lanes of traffic on Broadway while also providing a

showcase for urban transportation, the future Downtown L.A. Streetcar, and revitalization of Broadway." *Flackage* is, of course, the operative word, with a nice new one-sheet, complete with before and after images, and a "What's to Come" roster of future improvements, which include "new pedestrian lighting, street furniture, way-finding signage ... , plants and street trees, ... decorative paving materials ... , drainage and filtration system and more." At the top of the page is an artist's rendition of Broadway as it one day may be (and also—yes—as it once was): theater marquees lit and gleaming, sidewalks full of walkers, and in the middle of the scene a vintage Red Car, running along the pavement as if it had never disappeared. If a piece of me can't help but be cynical, another piece is equally compelled.

That's also my reaction to what is happening this evening: a showcase, CityLab: Making L.A., which is part of the second annual CityLab: Urban Solutions to Global Challenges conference, a two-day gathering for "global mayors and leading urban thinkers," cosponsored by the Aspen Institute, *The Atlantic*, and Bloomberg Philanthropies. The event begins with cocktails in the Spanish-Gothic lobby, beneath the vaulted ceilings and ornate plasterwork. This was once the broadcast home of Dr. Eugene Scott, the hat-wearing televangelist who preached out of the theater from 1990 until his death in 2005; I used to watch him on public access cable when I lived in New York. He is said, by Hillsman Wright of the Los Angeles Historic Theatre Foundation, to have left the place in "perhaps the most turn-key shape" of all the historic theaters on Broadway, but more to the point is what his stewardship—and now its aftermath—has to tell us about the changing face of L.A. Scott, after all, is a figure from a different city, in which downtown was widely regarded as a wasteland, a place, for all intents and purposes, to avoid. Here we see the Los Angeles that inspired the dystopian visions of *Falling Down* and *Blade Runner*, not to mention Kurt Russell's 1996 movie *Escape from L.A.* Here we see the Los Angeles of Mike Davis's *City of Quartz*, which imagines the city as one in which "the defense of luxury lifestyle is translated into a proliferation of new repressions in space and movement, undergirded by the ubiquitous 'armed response.'" L.A., *City of Quartz* continues, is obsessed "with physical security systems, and, collaterally, with the architectural policing of social boundaries," and is thus the embodiment of "a zeitgeist of urban restructuring, a master narrative in the emerging built environment of the 1990s." Still, if this was true in its own time, the city, as Christopher Hawthorne has written, "has changed markedly since the book appeared. It is fitfully trying to rediscover its public and shared spaces, and to build a comprehensive mass-transit system to thread them together.... We are at the beginning of a period in which the Metropolitan Transportation Authority, its coffers stuffed with $40 billion in Measure R transit funding, is poised to have a bigger effect on the built environment of Southern California than all the private developers combined. The city council earlier this year passed a bicycle master plan, for goodness sake."

This is the Los Angeles that the Making L.A. summit intends to highlight, a city in the process of recreating itself. If that means a little flackage, a little boosterism, then so be it—or so the prevailing wisdom seems to go. The night's participants include Kogi food truck chef Roy Choi and the mayor, although the real draw is a conversation between Rick Caruso and Los Angeles County Museum of Art Executive Director Michael Govan, titled "The Power of Place: Putting Culture on the (Urban) Map." It's ironic that Caruso and Govan, who, both together and independently, are working to reconfigure Mid-Wilshire, should be sitting on a downtown stage in a theater built around the same time as A.W. Ross first laid out the parameters of Miracle Mile. And yet, as always in Los Angeles, there are resonances, echoes, unlikely whispers of connection—despite Caruso's damning-by-faint-praise assessment of the Broadway reclamation project. "It's great," he says, "what's going on here, but it's fragile." The next day, a friend who was also in attendance wonders how much of the street he actually saw. "Can you imagine?" she asks. "Rick Caruso walking down Broadway?"—and I'm reminded of his comments *(You're not going to have crime, you're not going to have graffiti)* about the security, the sanctity, of the Grove. In order to succeed, Caruso suggests, the city will have to "activate" the space of downtown in much the same way as he has activated the Grove, that is, by hosting "more than three hundred events a year," although it is not clear, and he does not explain, how such a process might work in the less controlled environment of a public street. At the same time, listening to him and Govan, it's impossible not to see some sort of confluence between the changes on Broadway and those taking place in Miracle Mile. For one, there are those projected trolleys: the first a city project and the second a developer's fantasy. When asked about this, Caruso declares, "I think it's critical. L.A. is changing because we can't get around." I'm reminded once again of Huizar's press release *(boldly prioritizing people over vehicles)*, which offers both a rhetorical posture and the message we most need to hear. In that sense, there is a connection between his attempts and those of Caruso, both trying to push, in their own ways and for their own reasons, a sense of the city as communal, a series of (yes) shared environments.

If that sounds counterintuitive, it isn't really, although it depends on how we define the terms. For Huizar, the goal is renewal, revitalization, whereas for Caruso, it is, as it has ever been, the creation of place. As for Govan, he sits in the middle; during the eight years he's run the County Museum, he has sought to blend tradition and innovation, refocusing the museum's relationship to both the neighborhood and the city at large. "We need collective centers, even if they are symbolic," he argues, referring to the museum as a kind of temple, secular or otherwise. What he's getting at is something akin to scripted space, although, in this case on a level more aesthetic than commercial, in which experience is heightened in, for want of a better metaphor, a truly sacred way. As an example, Govan cites *Urban Light*, the lamppost installation that has opened the County Museum to Wilshire Boulevard, and in so doing, affected the dynamic of the street itself. "I did my research at the Grove," he jokes. "When I came to the Museum, the plan was to have an enclosed entry, but I made the decision to put the entrance outdoors. It was the beginning of my thinking about place. Whether you're talking about a real temple or a faux temple, the key is that it has to be iconic, a landmark people recognize and where they want to gather. In the most prosaic sense, you have to take your Facebook picture somewhere, which they do at three A.M. in front of *Urban Light*."

The following afternoon, I walk the ten blocks from my house to the County Museum, to talk with Govan in more detail. It's a Tuesday, last day of September, sky high and open, summer blue. Coming up Spaulding to Wilshire, I pass the parking lot that may soon be developed as a hundred thousand square foot wing of the museum—assuming, that is, that architect Peter Zumthor's proposed new building goes up as planned. First unveiled in 2013, the design has lately been adapted to address concerns raised by the Page Museum, which oversees the Tar Pits, about the continuing archeological work in Hancock Park. The original idea, for a structure that, according to Hawthorne, would "suggest the work of artist Jean Arp and architect Oscar Niemeyer along with the oozing shape of the tar pits," raised concerns about encroachment. "If I understand correctly," John Harris, the Page's chief curator, told the *Los Angeles Times* about the pits that lie closest to the County Museum, "this would all be under an overhang.... It would block off the light, the rain, and that affects the vegetation." Now, "Zumthor's black blob," which Hawthorne once described as "a muscular graphic form" that "would have floated on its expansive site—newly cleared with the proposed demolition of four existing County Museum gallery buildings—like an all-black abstract painting on a wide canvas," has been reimagined as "part of the boulevard and the public realm." Its most controversial feature is a glass-enclosed pedestrian bridge that crosses Wilshire, which supporters say will integrate the vista of the street, the sweep of it, into the experience of the museumgoer, although detractors warn that it will be like creating a freeway overpass over one of the city's signature boulevards.

As with many such debates, this one has the potential to become loaded, especially if we think of Wilshire as a model for the reframing of Los Angeles. Food trucks, public art, a vibrant and (Greg Hise aside) organic walking culture—it's like moving through the streets of not another city but a more heightened city, a city finding its form. On a strip of concrete in front of 5900 Wilshire, the Wende Museum and Archive of the Cold War has installed ten panels from the Berlin Wall. At the center are two portraits, one of John F. Kennedy and the other of Ronald Reagan, as if to indicate the bookends of its history. Along the sidewalk, office workers and museum-goers stop for Vietnamese food, deli fare, Mexi-terranean tacos, an explosion of cultural foment. "This," Jonathan Gold has written, "is Los

Angeles, where you hear a hundred different languages on the streets and smell the cooking of a thousand different food cultures, a city so diverse that the study of postmodern urbanism is often called the L.A. School for short, a city where it is possible not only to discover a new dish on an evening out but also an entirely new cuisine.... It's the way Los Angeles—the best Los Angeles—looks at the world." Here, we see the vision that the mayor made explicit from the stage of the United Artists Theatre, when he recommended, in response to a question about his favorite street meal: "Go to Wilshire, across from LACMA, and have one from each food truck."

Govan considers the County Museum an essential component of this process—and this process as essential to the museum. His office has windows that look onto the boulevard, as if to keep the relationship in mind. "You have to be an idiot not to see that this is a key piece of real estate in Los Angeles," he tells me, sitting at a long conference table, sipping from a bottle of water, comfortable in white dress shirt and light blue tie. "If there's a geographic center, halfway between the beach and downtown, between the Hollywood Hills and the 10, this is it. I'm not saying there isn't Pasadena, or the Valley and everything else, but even for them, as L.A. stretches all the way to Long Beach, this is the center, and you can see the pendulum that's swung." *Center* is an interesting word to use in Los Angeles: the word, perhaps, of an ex-New Yorker, which, Govan acknowledges, he is. But then, why not? I am one also, which is a big part of the reason I'm drawn to his vision of the boulevard, the museum campus, as epicentral (to borrow a word from Mike Davis) to the city's redevelopment. At the same time, Govan is not arguing for Manhattanization—at least not in terms Manhattan might recognize. He's talking more symbolically, more ... aesthetically, thinking about the city as a template, a canvas, and how we want to fill it in. That this reflects the history of Miracle Mile is part of the equation; indeed, we might say, a similar set of intentions motivated A.W. Ross when he bought his eighteen-acre strip of Wilshire (for $54,000) in 1921. "From the way you talk, A.W.," a friend purportedly told him, "one would think this is really a *miracle* mile"—and if this story is, as Nathan Masters has suggested, apocryphal, it's representative, as well. For all that Ross may have been more of a Caruso figure, his sensibility and Govan's coincide in interesting ways. For one thing, both are true believers. "I'm obviously an enthusiast," Govan admits. That's why, when he came to the County Museum, one of his first acts was to remake the museum's entrance, from the recessed set-back it had long been to something more open and engaged. "This was still a city street when I got here," he says, gesturing towards Ogden Drive, which no longer runs through the campus, but now dead-ends across the boulevard from *Urban Light.* "I got rid of the entry pavilion, with some consternation from my trustees, but if the Grove can be outside, we can be outside. Because they have to make money. If they can survive with an outdoor plaza, we can survive with an outdoor plaza. It's about the image it projects to everyone about the openness of the museum as a place."

Openness, of course, is what Wilshire lacked until the County Museum began to turn it around. In that regard, *Urban Light* is a key piece of the puzzle, a precipitating element. Among L.A.'s anomalies is that it is a city without a lot of landmarks; when Ahmed Ressam, the so-called millennium bomber, was arrested on December 14, 1999 in Port Angeles, Washington after trying to smuggle a Chrysler filled with explosives from Canada into the United States, his target was LAX. It's impossible (for me, anyway) to imagine another city in which the most obvious point of attack would be an airport, in which there is no symbol more potent or profound. "Everyone carries around a mental image of the place they inhabit," Govan insists. "Whether it's their bedroom or their house or their neighborhood. Or the metropolis. The distinctiveness itself is important, which is why, if you can create a thing that has layers of meaning inside it, that's what a great landmark is." What he's talking about is both iconography and spectacle; *Urban Light* fulfills both roles. As the putative entry point for the museum, it is a locus, a fulcrum, but it is also an installation that folds back on itself, distinctive and sardonic at once. On the one hand, the colonnade satirizes the solemnity of Greco-Roman architecture, the self-seriousness of the traditional museum. On the other, the fact that all 202 lampposts come from Los Angeles gives the project an unlikely authenticity. "These are Los Angeles streetlights from the 1920s and the 1930s," Govan says, "Greco-Roman inspired streetlights, and I always joke that if the Met in New York has its Greco-Roman temple façade, we have our faux façade, but actually it's real." I've never thought about the piece in quite these terms, but as Govan speaks, I get a sense of all these interlocking levels, the layers of meaning to which he refers.

The irony (or one of them) is that this installation almost didn't make it to Los Angeles; before the County Museum became interested, it looked as if it might end up at the Museum of Applied Arts in Vienna, which also co-owns West Hollywood's Schindler House. Now it seems not only inevitable, which is to say that it is difficult to imagine Wilshire Boulevard without it, but also like the advance guard in a move to turn the museum campus into quasi-public space. I say *quasi* because it is both public and not quite public, reliant on a 30-million dollar annual subsidy from L.A. County, but also on an array of private support. The Zumthor building offers a case in point; more than three-quarters of its 600-million dollar price tag will be raised from private donors, but its completion depends on 125 million dollars in county funds. Public/private, private/public, the great back-and-forth of Southern California, making even its most accessible spaces complicated, testing our understanding of the city and how it works. Although I walk through Hancock Park on an almost daily basis, on Wednesdays, I have to make adjustments: the museum is closed, its corner of the park gated off. I understand the logic, but still, I wonder: Is it possible to have a relationship part-time? This remains the challenge of a city that even now defines itself through the lens of the enormous village, although that is in the midst of a transition, which is another way of saying it is not yet here or there. "I agree," Govan notes, "that traditionally Los Angeles has a fear of shared spaces. But that was the lesson from the Grove: when you do it, people like it. I know that here, people like seeing two thousand people for Friday night jazz, and by the way, it changes generationally." What else is left us, then, except to build it incrementally, within existing structures, to let it take its course? Seen in such terms, perhaps, the expansion, or reinvention, of the County Museum can be regarded, not unlike the Grove, as another test case, an urban laboratory.

At heart is the ideal of place, whether public or quasi-public . . . or some other variation on the theme. It's not just *Urban Light* but what *Urban Light* signifies: the sacred or the heightened once again. At the same time, we live in a post-sacred age, which means that any such sensibility must be tempered—it is a temple, yes, but a postmodern one. Both landmark and spectacle, in other words. And yet, if this has a lot to do with irony, it's not irony as mockery but rather as an opening, a strategy for serious play. In Govan's estimation, *Urban Light* is both "a temple and it's not. It's a pop temple. It's art you can touch. It's made of enamel; you can hug it, you can take your picture kissing it. That tactility and spectacle, there's a constant back and forth between aspiration and the everyday." Something similar marks the other landmarks on the museum site, most notably Michael Heizer's *Levitated Mass.* Heizer was born and raised in Berkeley, the son of an archeologist; both experiences have influenced his work. In 1969 and 1970, he carved what Jori Finkel has described as "a pair of gashes into the Mormon Mesa, not far from Las Vegas"—a fifteen hundred foot long earth work called *Double Negative* that is both enormous and virtually invisible to the eye, at least at ground level. Owned and overseen by L.A.'s Museum of Contemporary Art, it is best perceived from above, like *Los Angeles: From Space.* In the aerial view, we see two long trenches, with the mesa in between them, tracing the extension of a broken line. On the ground, this gets more complicated, which is, of course, the whole idea. "There is nothing there, yet it is still a sculpture," Heizer has said, which highlights the essential conundrum: what defines the work is its emptiness, the removal of what once occupied the space. In that sense, we are being asked to face an absence, with all the uneasiness, the contradiction, this provokes. Where is the art, and what does it tell us? What is the message in its paradox?

As it turns out, these are the questions that much of Heizer's art confronts. His ongoing project *City*, more than forty years in the making, is a conglomeration of wedge-like steles and structures covering a location in the Nevada desert about the size of the National Mall in Washington, D.C. "As long as you're going to make a sculpture," he notes, "why not make one that competes with a 747, or the Empire State Building, or the Golden Gate Bridge?" The same might be said of *Levitated Mass*, a 340-ton diorite granite boulder suspended over a 456-foot concrete trench dug into the northwest corner of the County Museum campus, where it offers a symbolic counterweight to the Tar Pits, among other things. Part of the point is spectacle, an intention driven home during the rock's eleven-day journey, in March 2012, from a quarry in Riverside to the installation site. "I think people need a religious object," Heizer said of public reaction to the transport, which included, as Catherine Wagley reported in *LA Weekly*, "a 'Rockapalooza' party in Bixby Knolls [a neighborhood in Long Beach], where children made pet rocks and people consumed Rockstar Energy Drinks," and culminated in a late-night, slow-speed passage along Wilshire Boulevard. Much discussed, much delayed, covered by both local and national media, the movement of the boulder became a phenomenon in its own right, a piece of public performance art. "In Los Angeles," environmentalist Char Miller observed, "where mobility is so important, the idea of movement, and closing down streets, may have been more impressive than the art installation itself, which is static." Little wonder, then, that once *Levitated Mass* was installed, it seemed anticlimactic; there is a difference, after all, between a contained event, especially one that stirs up such excitement, and the day-in, day-out reality of art as monument.

Still, if anticlimax is, perhaps, an inevitable response, it is also part of the challenge of the piece. Spectacle, monument … the more we live with it, the more familiar it becomes, the more it represents a kind of necessary double vision, internal and external, by turns part of the imagination and of the world. Irony again, or perhaps a way in which the city is transformed. My own experience may be instructive. I was out of town for the rock's slow ride down Wilshire, although I had anticipated it for months. I wanted to see what it would look like, a giant boulder juxtaposed against the temporary city, an expression of the prehistoric brought to life. I wanted to be awed, to be pulled outside myself, to consider this place not only on human but also geologic terms. That is the key contradiction of Los Angeles—or this section of it, anyway—a contradiction to which we all must keep returning, the juxtaposition of the ancient, the prehuman, against the thin sheen of the city we have built. It's what the Tar Pits insist we recognize, with their mix of archeology and contrivance, which is (come to think of it) a pretty good description of Heizer's aesthetic as well. "It's a play with spectacle and observation and definitions," Govan tells me, voice rising with excitement, face opening like that of a precocious child.

> And since the museum is also something that covers ancient to modern cultures, I can easily read it as: *The rock is as ancient as it comes.* Mike Heizer always says his work is about—we live in primordial and modern times simultaneously. So how do we court both? He said, "Do you want this rock?" And I pictured the thing rolling down Wilshire Boulevard, and I said, "Damn right I want that rock." That's exactly what I had in mind. I want to make a sense of place.

Not only that, but "pretty much every culture has moved big rocks from somewhere else, because that's part of the marking and place making." In that sense, it's a monolith, an obelisk, albeit one with which, not unlike *Urban Light*, we interact.

Such an interaction takes place across both time and space, which is also the essence of a neighborhood. We live here, we walk through, we define ourselves in terms of our passage through this campus, through these streets. I'll be honest: I was disappointed with *Levitated Mass* when it opened; it was smaller than I had expected, less profound. I wanted it to be ten times its size, or one hundred, so massive it provoked a kind of claustrophobia. Instead, the boulder sat in the center of an empty sandlot the size of two football fields, where it appeared, at certain times of day, in certain lights, almost like an afterthought. *This is it?* I remember thinking the first time I saw it. Now, I'd argue that's precisely the idea. Like the Tar Pits, which I walk past all the time without overtly noticing, its purpose is to function as both spectacle and background, to unsettle us just slightly, on a cellular as much as a conscious level, by expressing what let's call the limits of our power. By power, I don't mean political so much as existential, a distinction about which Govan is explicit, framing *Levitated Mass* as an alternate universe take on Cleopatra's Needle, the ancient Egyptian obelisk that sits behind the Metropolitan Museum of Art in Manhattan's Central Park. Like Heizer's boulder, the Needle caused a frenzy when it was brought to New York in 1880, although for decades now, a century, it has blended into the cityscape of which it is a part. At the same time, it possesses none of the self-reflecting irony, the recognition of our evanescence, that the rock embodies at is core. "It's not just the gravitas or beauty of an image," Govan says,

> It's that there are indeed multiple approaches to reading it. When New York wanted the Needle, which they took in complicated times of government in Egypt, when you could extract it—it was literally obelisk envy, of Paris, Rome. Culture equaled a thing you brought from Egypt. New York wanted to be a world-class city in that way. A century later, in Los Angeles, it's not an obelisk that stands tall like a phallus, it's a negative space. It's a parable of observation, in the sense that it's a heavy object that has this sense of mass, but you can observe it not only from every side but underneath. You can see the bottom of the sculpture. So it's a parable, or a process of observation, of close observation, not one of the projection of power.

Something similar, or so the argument goes, may be at the center of the proposed new County Museum building, which, initially at least, sought to echo the Tar Pits and to integrate their ancient shape. A more recent iteration, the *Los Angeles Times* reported in March 2015, is "noticeably more angular and muscular" than the earlier "free-flowing, biomorphic design." That both shapes are also contrivances—remember, the tar lake was only dug out a hundred years ago—is both appropriate (whatever form it ultimately takes, after all, the building, too, will be a construction, an attraction) and yet one more layer of irony. In a piece for the *Architectural Record* website, Sarah Williams Goldhagen digs into Zumthor's process, reminding us that "designs are not buildings. Designs are not even half buildings. Designs are promises, flashbulbs of an idea." The reference is to the bridge across Wilshire, which, depending on your perspective, is either an assault or an enhancement, but in any case represents a far more direct assertion of the museum upon the street than even *Urban Light* suggests. What does this mean, this imposition of the private on the public? How does it change our experience of the street? These questions seem especially important given the other changes in the boulevard over the last several years, as well as those that will come when the subway arrives. Zumthor, who is Swiss, has been criticized for not "getting" Los Angeles, although he did teach at the Southern California Institute of Architecture, in downtown's arts district, in 1988. More to the point, Goldhagen suggests, is his belief (with a focus not dissimilar to Heizer's) that "the city matters, but so does the Ice Age site on which LACMA sits." Goldhagen continues: "Looking at art, Zumthor has said, can be a profound, even transcendental experience. For Los Angeles, Zumthor is less focused on the perpetual transience of the city than he is on the permanent—on what was there in Los Angeles before there even was a Los Angeles." What he's presenting, then, may be a deeper integration, in which the human scale of Wilshire begins to recognize, and to mirror, the natural landscape of which it is a part. This has always been the disconnect in Southern California, between its edenic myths and its more elemental realities, between the history of forgetting and the forgetting of history. "Those tar pits are the soul of that site," Zumthor declares, and he's right, as they are in many ways the soul of the city itself. It's no coincidence that, in works as disparate as Helena María Viramontes's 1995 novel *Under the Feet of Jesus* and the 1997 blockbuster movie *Volcano*, tar is a metaphor for dislocations social and geologic. "Black bubbles erasing him," Viramontes writes. "Finally the eyes. Blankness. Thousands of bones, the bleached white marrow of bones. Splintered bone pieced together by wire to make a whole, surfaced bone." There is erasure here, but equally the inevitability of that first place, that elemental center, that prehistoric world that underlies the floating human grid. "No fingerprint or history, bone," Viramontes continues. "No lava stone. No story or family, bone."

The paradox is that the tar, or its by-products, nearly derailed the subway—in fact, *did* derail the subway for more than twenty years. On March 24, 1985, Ross Dress for Less, a discount clothing store a few blocks east of Fairfax on Third Street (directly across the street from the site that would become the Grove), exploded after a methane build-up in its basement, the entire building "rising just slightly with an enormous burp," notes William L. Fox in *Making Time: Essays on the Nature of Los Angeles*, "then settling back down, although twenty-two people were injured." In the aftermath, Henry Waxman, who represented the district in Congress, sponsored legislation that banned the use of federal funds for subway construction in the area, a ban that wasn't lifted until 2007. We can talk all we want about the wisdom (or lack thereof) of digging subway tunnels in a land-scape as unstable as Southern California. "Tunnels are the safest place during an earthquake because tunnels move as one unit with the ground," insists Metro's Krishniah Murthy, although the system has not yet had to ride out anything bigger than Northridge, which at magnitude 6.7 was terrifying, disruptive... and yet packed only a fraction of the force of the so-called Big One most Californians dread. Who knows what would happen if a 7.8 were to strike? Perhaps Waxman was right, although by this point, we've moved beyond such concerns and into the realm of aesthetics and policy. "We've got the best weather in the world and we put people underground," sneers Rick Caruso, a long-time critic of the subway, even as he acknowledges that Los Angeles is changing because people can't get around. "That's why it's critical to connect neighborhoods," he adds, arguing once again for his trolley, the glue, as it were, that he believes would help the neighborhood cohere.

Whether or not this is the case remains a matter of conjec-ture; as a friend likes to remind me, it's only ten blocks from the County Museum to the Grove, no more than fifteen minute's walking time. I do it a few times a month, passing through the museum campus to Sixth Street, then west on Sixth and north on Fairfax to Third. It is hardly the prettiest saunter in the neighborhood, along the narrow sidewalks that skirt the walled-in edge of Park La Brea, but it's not without a certain oddball charm. There are people, buses, a sense of streets that are, that have been, lived in; if nothing else, it comes with a low-level urban buzz. In any event, the trolley "is not happening any time soon," admits Govan, although "with the subway coming in and LACMA growing, it becomes more relevant." A key issue remains where to put it. "Traffic on Fairfax is a disaster," Govan says, "so the county and the city will never put a trolley there." One potential solution involves running tracks through Park La Brea, although this comes with problems of its own. Park La Brea, after all, is gated, landscaped, set back from the surrounding streets as if it were an island on the land. First developed in the 1940s, influenced by Le Corbusier, it has become another of L.A.'s strange nonlandmark landmarks, most notable (perhaps) for being there. As long as I've lived in the neighborhood, I have thought of it as a roadblock, an impediment, the place where the street comes to die. For Govan, this is the whole idea. "Fencing off Park La Brea—they have to change that," he insists, although he recognizes the difficulties. "It's all private, and I think it would take a pretty big act to change the permissions they got to build the fence. So they would have to want to do it. We're not trying to force anything." And yet, the vision he articulates is an enticing one, in which the property is redeveloped, opened up. Rather than remaining behind walls and gates, it would blur into the broader community, not unlike the museum, with its ongoing reconceptualization, its integration of the street. "I don't know Park La Brea," Govan says, "I'm not trying to take it over" ... but then he is off and running: "Maybe we could create this north-south access, with walking traffic and retailers. It could improve real estate values, help with historic buildings. And between the twenty million people visiting the Grove and the subway stop here, think of the street traffic. That would be fantastic. So maybe the trolley could come through Park La Brea."

What Govan's really describing is density, which is coming (has come) to Los Angeles, with or without its gates and walls. That's the charm, for me, of this corner of the city, with its horizontal downtown and its public art, its sense of the boulevard as

a "great street." It is Wilshire, in other words, that is the destination, the street as landmark, or experience. Of course, as Govan
notes, "when we talk about density in L.A., we're not talking
about the overall packed density of Manhattan. Manhattan is a
small island. Los Angeles is a massive horizontal surface. So
you're not going to get density everywhere." He's right; even at
its most urbanized, L.A. remains loosely packed. It's tempting to
consider this in terms of sprawl, although it's more accurate, I
think, to read it as the function of a decentered urban landscape,
in which even downtown is just one in a series of contiguous districts, isolated and connected all at once. That is why the subway remains so essential, despite environmental analyses that
indicate, the *Los Angeles Times* reports, "only limited relief on
Wilshire and nearby surface streets and little or no relief for the
area's freeways." I don't mean to suggest that these analyses are
incorrect; one rail line (or even two if we count the Expo Line,
which will reach Santa Monica by way of Culver City in 2016)
won't, *can't*, make that much difference to the toxic gridlock of
the streets. And yet, I want to tell you that this doesn't matter,
that the subway may be less important as transit system than as
metaphor. Don't get me wrong: I'm as eager as anyone (more
eager, I would wager) to travel the basin via underground railroad, any time of day or evening, fourteen minutes from the
County Museum to downtown. I've been waiting for it for a generation, would use it now if the expansion were completed, and
regret, then and now, my inability to take a train to hear Govan
and Caruso at the United Artists, registering it as a lost opportunity, symbol (still) of our dislocation, the distance between
where we wish to be and where we are. At the same time, I'm
skeptical, it's in my nature to be skeptical, especially when it
comes to the promises L.A. makes. As early as the 1880s, Carey

McWilliams writes in *Southern California Country*, "it began to be said that Southern Californians 'irrigate, cultivate, and exaggerate'"—an observation that lingers even now. Back to the future, forward to the past: the story that the city tells about itself.

Does that sound like yet another whisper of Los Angeles exceptionalism, the sensibility I want most to avoid? Maybe so, although I think it's more complicated than that. For McWilliams, who coined the phrase, exceptionalism was a double-edged sword, connected to what we might regard (without irony or subtext) as manifest destiny. "Californians," he argues in *California: The Great Exception*, "are more like the Americans than the Americans themselves." And later: "California has always occupied, in relation to other regions, much the same relation that America has occupied toward Europe: it is the great catch-all, the vortex at the continent's end into which elements of America's diverse population have been drawn, whirled around." Such a sentiment, suggests Mitchell Schwarzer in *Harvard Design Magazine*, predicts Wallace Stegner's famous "California was America only more so," which also cuts both ways. On the one hand, each of these writers is referring to energy, innovation, the constant cycles of a boom economy; on the other, to the exploitation of resources and human beings. "The state is always off balance, stretching itself precariously," McWilliams lamented, and sixty-five years later, it's not hard to hear that imbalance echoed in the rhetoric of civic leaders like the mayor, who claims that the subway "will help people get to where they need to go, cut traffic and boost the economy," or his counterpart in Santa Monica (where, it must be said, *this* train isn't going), who told the *Los Angeles Times*, "if the car is king of L.A., then the Purple Line will be the queen of L.A." Queen of L.A. The City of Our Lady the Queen of the Angels. As Richard Rodriguez noted in 1992:

"Americans have their leveling ways: La Ciudad de Nuestra Señora de los Ángeles de Porciuncula has become, in one hundred years, L.A."

All the same, can I say that I want to believe it, that this is the city (or a version of it) in which I want to live? Can I indulge in some Keatsian negative capability, hold two opposing ideas in my head? Yes, I am skeptical about the effects of the subway, about ridership, about whether it will alleviate the gridlock, and certainly about what happens in an earthquake. Even so, I look forward to its arrival, to the changes it will bring to my relationship with the city, to its sense of depth. I am skeptical, too, about Zumthor's design for the County Museum, which in a recent computer-generated image appears a bit flat, a bit low-slung, its bridge close in upon the boulevard, its western edge too near *Urban Light.* At the same time, how can I not be drawn to Govan's notion of the museum as "the park for the neighborhood. For the world, too, but for the neighborhood specifically. That was the idea, that eventually you can walk your dog through the museum because you can see art though the glass and walk through the park, and the museum is in the park." As for the overpass, he says, "Everyone asks, 'Will it be dark under there?' Would we build it if it were going to be dark? This isn't a highway overpass. We're talking about twenty-two feet in the air, we're talking about glass and light and art." In regard to its impact on Wilshire, there is a kink, a slight hiccup, in the boulevard between Spaulding and Stanley Avenues—"so sightlines converge." He goes on, rolling now, swept up in the vision: "It's actually an ideal point for a cross, for a visual marking of Wilshire, because you see the long lines out. It makes the boulevard a monument, which it is. And there'll be a restaurant with glass looking at *Urban Light* and you'll be able to see through the building, right to Sixth Street, right through the building because it's all open and glass. You'll be able to see the Page Museum from the main plaza. So it's anything but constraining. In fact, it's going to be like lifting a blockage out of the site."

Glass and light and art, the integration of street and subway, a vista through which you can walk your dog. Street life, in other words, although at the same time something more and less than that, which brings back all the city's paradoxes, imprinted, like footprints, loosely on the shifting, prehistoric ground. As for the Zumthor project, it seeks to function, at least in part, as something of a mirror, regardless of the ongoing evolution of its design. What we see in its gaze is our complexity, our inscrutability, and (equally important) those of the earth itself. We see the curious mix of contrived and elemental, our own construction beside the ancient tar. "It's by being out of synch with the ongoing present, or what we refer to as 'real time,' through experiencing the past and imagining the future," William Fox writes, "that we're able to perceive where we are, what our place is." This is exactly the sensation the Tar Pits provoke. And yet, Fox continues, "almost everyone, except for the kids in the LACMA parking lot, walks too fast to notice the tar oozing up through the asphalt or, seeing it, fails to consider what it means." Little wonder, then, that in *Volcano*—inspired, perhaps, by Waxman's concerns over the Ross Dress for Less explosion—"the construction of a subway tunnel was the fictional pretext leading to the eruption of the La Brea Tar Pits."

You can read such a plot point in a couple of different ways: as an example of the silliness of Hollywood, or as an expression of the apocalyptic impulse that has defined L.A. pop culture since there was an L.A. pop culture, a fantasy of devastation on the grand scale. In *Ecology of Fear: Los Angeles and the Imagination of*

Disaster, Mike Davis catalogues 138 films and novels (including *Volcano*) in which the city is destroyed—and that's only though 1998. Such a list reveals something about our unease with the volatility of this landscape, the elemental underpinnings of a city that can feel conditional even in its densest neighborhoods. I've spent a lot of time thinking about this in the years I've lived here, the psychology of the disaster zone. This afternoon, however, as I leave Govan's office and make my way back out to Wilshire, I find myself reflecting in far more pedestrian terms. It's been a few hours, and the sun has sunk below the midpoint of the sky; I turn east and wander beyond the bend where the overpass will go and watch the boulevard extend. To my right, the Craft Museum, to my left, the artificial shape of the tar lake, like Park La Brea, sequestered behind a fence with those plaster mammoths struggling on the shore. I can see myself here at many ages, six and thirty-six and fifty-three. I can see my children, or the afterimage of my children, rolling down the slope that presses against the Page Museum, climbing on the statues of the sloth and the short-faced bear. It is my history, our history, the history Los Angeles claims to forget. It is what roots us here. In front of a bench, a man plays the blues on a banjo; as I pass, he nods at me. I encounter him most days when I walk through this park, another of the loops by which I mark my place in this city, a walkabout, a songline, a way for me to meander my universe into being.

And I know that this is just a passing fancy, but today it all feels real to me in a way I can't quite name. Not lasting, never lasting, but connected, as if I can walk a bridge between the present and the past. A bridge that stretches across Wilshire, a bridge by which we come to some acceptance, to sacred ordinariness. This is my neighborhood, my community; as was true for La Brea Woman, it is where I live. And if she is just a facsimile, then I am one also, a conglomeration of my influences. I drift around the park, cross the lawn where in the summer there are salsa concerts, move out to the plaza of the museum. In the near distance, *Levitated Mass* reddens, pale as watercolor, in the sunlight, while before me *Urban Light* marks the border of the boulevard. As always, there are tourists snapping pictures, children pressing up against the lampposts, the imprint of a landmark, the way the city grows into itself. On the facing sidewalk, I see the subway site, construction on the station, and for a moment, I want to live forever, to experience Los Angeles as it will be in forty years, fifty, in a century, to engage with the urban landscape it becomes. This too is a fantasy: of a neighborhood that works on many levels, cars and trains and walkers flowing in and out of public/private spaces like the tar beneath our feet. And yet, why not? What else is a city but a dream in three dimensions, inhabited by succeeding generations who create identity in the muscle memory of its streets? What else is a city but an imaginatorium, where the surface, *the public record*, is constantly collapsing into the interior landscape, the streets as markers, territorial or otherwise, the building blocks, the triggers, of identity? That is how cities develop, that is how they evolve. "The Boulevard itself," Reyner Banham reminds us, "was the creation of years of ad hoc subdivisions, beginning with a quarter-mile stretch west of the present MacArthur Park laid out in 1895 by the ineffable Gaylord Wilshire." Little more than a century later, I cross it heading south, a part of my daily peregrination, in a city that neither Wilshire nor (for that matter) Ross would recognize, and make my way through "streets devoid of meaning to the driver"—but not, I want to tell you, to the walker who, like me, is where he or she belongs.

A Walker, in the City

It troubled me that I could speak in the fullness of my
own voice only when I was alone on the streets,
walking about.

Alfred Kazin

On a Saturday in early October, I drive to my son's apartment in
Koreatown, walk with him the four blocks to Wilshire and Western, where we take a Purple Line train downtown. The day is
warm, the tail end of another heat wave, and as we wander the
sidewalks of his neighborhood, I find myself confronting, once
again, the sensation of existing in both the present and the past.
When he was little, we used to do this once or twice a month: park
in the ten-hour lot between Wilshire and Sixth Street, ride the
train to Pershing Square, where we would emerge and cross the
street to Angels Flight, and spend an hour or so traveling up and
down. Back then, a decade and a half ago, the subway was just a
whisper, just a promise, built—prior to the current expansion, the
most recent work on this line ended with the opening of the North
Hollywood station, in 2000—but not yet integrated into any vision
the city might have of itself. For us then, the subway was more or
less a theme park ride, on which, for three dollars, we could get an

all-day pass, the public transportation equivalent of the old Disneyland E ticket. All the same, it offered a glimpse of where (we hoped) Los Angeles might be going: the multidimensional city that was, too often, invisible above the ground. It's been some time since there were ten-hour lots here; where we once parked is now the site of a high-rise, although the area has long been dense. "By 1928," writes Nathan Masters of Wilshire and Western, "more automobiles passed through here than through any other intersection in the nation." That was three years before construction of the Pellissier building and the Wiltern Theatre (originally called the Warner Western) created a deco landmark, twelve stories of aquamarine terra cotta on a diagonal to the intersection, like some kind of cousin to the Eastern building downtown.

Like many of L.A.'s classic buildings, the Wiltern suffered decades of neglect. In the 1970s, it was nearly demolished on two occasions—indeed, would have been demolished were it not for the Los Angeles Conservancy. By the early 1980s, it had been stripped of its vintage fixtures and parts of the ceiling had caved in. For a glimmer of the theater in this era, check out the 1983 film *Get Crazy*, a satire about the last night of a fabled rock-and-roll concert hall. Much of the movie was shot at the Wiltern, and as Malcolm McDowell (who played a parodic, Mick Jagger-inspired singer named Reggie Wanker) remembers, "We trashed it just before they restored it. They knew we were going to do it, so they didn't mind." Hollywood again, with its assertion of the city as disposable, as film set, *most photographed and least remembered*. But even more, I think, *Get Crazy* offers a bit of documentary evidence, images of L.A. as it was and is no longer, another artifact from the *Blade Runner* days.

Koreatown is something of a misnomer; although it does have a significant Korean American population ("one-third of all

Koreans living in the county," report Leonard and Dale Pitt), it is a majority Latino neighborhood. To the south, it abuts Pico-Union, among the city's roughest communities. This rendered it central to the divisions that marked Los Angeles in the 1980s and 1990s, and provoked its most apocalyptic fantasies. In 1992, less than a decade past *Get Crazy*, the area became a flashpoint of the Rodney King riots, after years of tension between Korean Americans and African Americans. "The nation's largest Korean American community is grim, armed, and determined to repel racial violence in its riot-scarred corner of the city," Seth Mydans wrote in *The New York Times*. "One of the most gripping and, increasingly, controversial television images of the violence was a scene of two Korean merchants firing pistols repeatedly from a military stance. The image seemed to speak of race war, and of vigilantes taking the law into their own hands." I'm reminded of Richard Rayner, who, in his essay "Los Angeles," recalls meeting a "smart Korean gentleman" and watching from the Silverlake hills as the city burned. "He remarked with a world weary air," Rayner notes, "that he had a business in the mid-Wilshire district, right next door to the Sears building, which now appeared to be ablaze. He wasn't going to defend it, though he knew some of his countrymen had armed themselves with shotguns and machine guns in Koreatown. But they were shopkeepers and he—he shrugged, a little apologetically—was not a shopkeeper. 'Nor am I Clint Eastwood,' he said. 'I pay America lots and lots of taxes so I don't have to be.'"

Clint Eastwood, Michael Douglas, Harrison Ford as Rick Deckard: these are the touchstones of another city, another time. A more relevant signifier today is Roy Choi, who grew up, in part, in the neighborhood and, with his Kogi food truck, which sells tacos filled with Korean barbeque, has come to embody the border-blurring aesthetic, culinary or otherwise, of contemporary Los Angeles. Choi's newest venture, a hotel on Wilshire six blocks east of Western called the Line, means to convert an old event and party space into a more three-dimensional experience. "No one had really done a hotel celebrating L.A. as this ethnic melting pot," observes Andrew Zobler, whose Sydell Group raised fifty million dollars to develop the property. Whether or not the Line succeeds, the idea is emblematic of how the city has begun to see itself. Koreatown is a good example; perhaps because of the subway, or the renovated Wiltern, or the food truck culture, it has become more diverse than it ever was. Think about my son: twenty years old, working, sharing an apartment with a roommate, in a building erected eighty years ago. He is here because he likes it, likes the mix, the feel of it, because it is urban on the most traditional terms. He doesn't drive, travels via bus and subway, interacts with the city in the way I used to wish I could, when I started wandering Wilshire Boulevard a generation ago. Today, as we make our passage to the Wilshire/Western station, we see all the elements of this complex urban landscape—elderly men and women pulling shopping caddies; another father and son, younger than us, off to shoot hoops at a schoolyard; a pair of twentysomethings on their bicycles: all of it so ordinary, so nondescript, I might not even notice, were we anywhere other than Los Angeles. No one has had to build it, or perhaps it's more accurate to say that it did not emerge out of a unified plan. Like Mid-Wilshire—even to some extent like downtown—it is the product of a series of overlapping agendas and priorities, developers, public transport, and (yes) members of the community, adapting the neighborhood to their own ends.

I'm not naïve about this process; I understand that the Line is an investment, that it will live or die as per the bottom line. Still, a luxury hotel in Koreatown? If that's not a symbol of some sort, I don't know what is. The same is true of the subway, which my son and I use now not as we once did, for the novelty of riding, but in the way in which, like all transit lines, it is intended: for connectivity. This afternoon, the destination is Grand Central Market to grab lunch and then meander through downtown. Just another Saturday that could be anywhere, a city experienced at human scale. Even so, that's the whole idea, isn't it—that none of this is, or will be, exceptional anymore? We use our TAP cards, pass through the turnstiles, wait on the platform for the train. All around us, the city pollinates: mothers with children, teen-agers goofing on each other, tourists unsure of where to go. In his 1973 essay "Autopia," Cees Nooteboom records the disasso-ciation of "sitting in a bus on my way to the [city] center." He writes, "I travel across the map and make little arrows and crosses for the day when I can drive myself." Underground, there is no map, except that of the stations; it is the city distilled to its purest essence, geography in outline form. All that matters is the speed of the passage, the proximity it engenders or antici-pates. This is what the freeways once must have been like, Santa Monica to Pasadena in twenty minutes, but if I have occasion-ally known that sensation late in the evening, midnight, one A.M., the road as empty as a river, it is no longer the prevailing narrative. Sitting on the train, I am aware again of the past to which we are returning, back to a city of neighborhoods.

Downtown, we wander through the market, deciding what we want. I get a bagel and lox, my son a plate of tacos; we take them to the tables lining Broadway, eat in the shadow of the traf-fic's rush. This is Jose Huizar's fantasy, people dining curbside as in Paris or Manhattan, a city that "boldly prioritizes people over vehicles." And yet, our table is too close to the street, to the congestion that has only gotten worse since this lane was shut down to accommodate diners, making me wonder what will happen when and if the streetcar finally arrives. Even now, as I am looking for a kind of reconciliation, Los Angeles provokes these dislocations in me. The city I live in and the city I want to live in, by turns horizontal and vertical, sprawling and contained. Over the summer, my wife and I met friends for dinner one Saturday night on Spring Street; after we were finished, we wandered over to the Varnish, a backroom bar on Sixth Street, built into the rear of Cole's. Here, we have a place that reminds us of the weight of time; Cole's has occupied the same space, in the old Pacific Electric Building (once the terminal of the Pacific Electric Railway), since 1908. A sign outside calls it "Los Angeles' oldest public house," although that doesn't refer to the Varnish, which opened in 2009. Layers again, past and present colliding, historic core reimagined, reinvented on contemporary terms. This is not only true of L.A. but also of cities across the country, where once derelict downtowns have been reinvigorated, revived. Call it ersatz, call it artisanal—the Varnish is both, of course, a fake speakeasy selling expensive designer drinks—even if I'm not sure such labels are relevant, at least when it comes to Los Angeles. In the years after I first moved here, when I was desperate to understand the city, I used to talk about its shapelessness, which paradoxically gave it a shape that I could see. *Order out of chaos* was how I liked to put it, but if that was useful to me then (and still is, to some extent), I've come to see the city through a convex lens. That night in downtown, the streets were jammed with hundreds if not thousands of people, most of them young and looking for action, although it would be hard to say how many were residents. I have a former student who spent many years living just a block or so from here, on

Main Street. "To gauge downtown's resurgence," she once suggested, "look for dogs." She's right: people don't bring their dogs to work, and they don't bring them when they go clubbing on a Saturday night. This same student also liked to tell me that the most effective measure of the economic or social status of a neighborhood has to do with whether the urine in the gutter is of the canine or the human kind.

There's still plenty of human urine on downtown's sidewalks, although less, perhaps, than there once was. But there is also a large population of dogs, which suggests something profound about the ways the city changes, large and small. That night with my wife and our friends, I was reminded of Soho, in Manhattan, in the late 1970s, when it was still borderline, an artists' neighborhood, in the process of being transformed. I don't want to push the Los Angeles/New York comparison, nor to imply that such transformations are necessarily or entirely for the good. By the time I moved to Soho in 1985, I had to fight my way through crowds of tourists every weekend; that shift was a reason (if not the major one), we moved to Los Angeles in 1991. I'm no fan of gentrification, and I don't want downtown to become a shopping mall. At the same time, there is something stirring about seeing the streets so full, especially in a district that as recently as six years ago was a city of the dead once it grew dark. I remember, in late October 2008, just before the presidential election, coming to the Orpheum to see a show by Patti Smith. Walking up Broadway to my car after the concert, it was as if a plague had struck, leaving only ghosts pushing shopping carts, dressed in rags. This was how I felt, for a decade or more, whenever I came downtown: as if I were entering the underworld. "This place?" I say to my son, gesturing at the Los Angeles Theatre Center, which occupies a former bank building on Spring

Street between Fifth and Sixth. "Twenty years ago, I'd spend entire performances worrying about whether we would get jumped on the way back to the car." Is that an exaggeration? Yes and no. Downtown L.A. in the 1990s was the most terrifying urban landscape I have seen. Is it any wonder then that each time I am here now a part of me can't help but marvel, even as another part of me is thrilled that I no longer have to marvel, that this, too, is becoming a part of the city's ordinary tapestry?

My son and I cut back to Broadway, walk south through the Theater District, which is a centerpiece of Huizar's Bring Back Broadway campaign. Most of these theaters have long been shuttered, and it's unclear what is planned for them, other than the cosmetic improvement of refurbished marquees. At the same time, Broadway remains a ground zero of sorts for the culture clash between the new downtown, embodied by the professionals who have moved into lofts and high-rises, and the long-tenured merchants of the *mercado*. "On one side, I like the idea [of the redevelopment]," a woman who worked at a Broadway bridal shop told the *Los Angeles Times* in 2008. "The only thing is that I don't think they want our types of businesses." As with Grand Central Market, the results are not yet in. We pass the Los Angeles Theater and the Palace, stop at Loew's State Theatre, an old vaudeville and movie house on the corner of Seventh Street, opened in 1921. The last film was screened here in 1998, but for the last six years, it's been a Spanish-language church, and since services are in session, we go in. For moment, I feel as if we are trespassing, as if we are someplace we shouldn't be. This is the history of Los Angeles, of California, in a nutshell: appropriation, usurpation, erasure of the past. Nobody but me, however, seems to notice, and as we pass through the lobby and into the auditorium, we hear not a word nor see a gesture to suggest we

ought to go away. There is no preacher, just a movie screen on
which a sermon is projected at low volume. A handful of wor-
shippers sit scattered in the theater's seats. My son murmurs
something about the bones of the building, how it might look
after renovation, the dome of the ceiling, the depth of the stage.
I can't help thinking of the United Artists, which not all that long
ago was also used as a church. Now it's been restored to its historic glory—although who, really, gets to say what our historic
glory is?

Eventually, we end up at that reconstructed palace, jewel in
the crown of the district, or so the flackage would have us
believe. My own feelings are a bit more complicated, but on a
Saturday afternoon, the sidewalks are blissfully free of hipsters,
no sign of any kind of scene. We wander around the back, in the
shadow of the "Jesus Saves" sign, on a two-block street called
Blackstone Court. At the northern end, I can see the façade of
the Eastern building, less imposing at street level, like a building
in which anyone could work or live. My son climbs a fire escape
and catwalk, looking for a point of access, but the United Artists
is locked. And I know I should tell him not to, but why get in the
way of a good thing? The afternoon is so relaxed, so quiet, and
we are just wandering the city, staking out our place. Walkabout
again, Dreaming tracks, although we are not Aboriginals, or at
least I'm not. My son was born here, he was raised here, although
until the last year or so, he has never felt any particular connection to L.A. He always wanted to live in New York, or San Francisco, some other urban landscape, but lately he has come to an
accommodation, finding a center in a city without a center, a set
of markers, territorial or otherwise. Cities have lives of their
own, by turns organic and inorganic; they are vast multi-cell
organisms pushed in any number of directions at once. We are

in Los Angeles at a moment when the shape that it is taking, or that part of it is taking—there is still all that endless diffusion, houses set back from the boulevards, just take a drive on Sunset if you don't believe me, all those sweeping curves and isolated mansions, or into the flats of Van Nuys, Valley Village, Palms— is amenable to us. Growing up and not out, the city is at its limits, reconfiguring its past, its heritage, back to the future again.

From Blackstone Court, we walk west to Figueroa, then north past the site of the Wilshire Grand. The skyscraper that is in the process of going up here, built by Korean Air, will be, at eleven hundred feet and seventy-three stories, the tallest building west of the Mississippi when it is completed in 2017. It's a key component of the (re-)developing Figueroa Corridor—although what is the Figueroa Corridor? Just one small piece of a street that runs for thirty miles, from San Pedro to Pasadena, a metaphor for the city's neighborhoods, its density, and its sprawl. Such distances are hard to wrap one's mind around, are *one reason the place exhilarates some people, and floods others with an amorphous unease.*

And I'm thinking now of all the ways Los Angeles confounds us, the multitudes it contains. And I'm thinking now of how the city changes, how it has already, in some fundamental fashion, changed. My son and I make our way to Metro Center, Seventh and Flower, one long block to the east. Our walk through downtown has spelled out some kind of story in the letters inscribed by our feet. A story? More a song, a set of impressions; L.A. remains elusive to me even now. So much of what I want I have to wait for, so much remains distant, out of reach. By the time the subway reaches Westwood, I'll be in my seventies. Will I still live here (or still be living)? There's no way to know. As we ride back beneath the streets, I can't help but note the echoes, my history and that of the city intertwined. Los Angeles, the City of Our Lady the Queen of the Angels, la Ciudad de Nuestra Señora de los Ángeles de Porciuncula. This is where I am.

ABOUT THE AUTHOR

David L. Ulin is the author, most recently, of the novella *Labyrinth*. His other books include *The Lost Art of Reading: Why Books Matter in a Distracted Time* and *The Myth of Solid Ground: Earthquakes, Prediction, and the Fault Line Between Reason and Faith,* selected as a best book of 2004 by the *Chicago Tribune* and the *San Francisco Chronicle*. He has also edited three anthologies: *Another City: Writing from Los Angeles, Cape Cod Noir,* and the Library of America's *Writing Los Angeles: A Literary Anthology,* which won a California Book Award. A 2015 Guggenheim Fellow, he is book critic, and former book editor, of the *Los Angeles Times*.